Finding Your Voice

How to Speak Your Heart's True Faith

JIM DANT

© 2013

Published in the United States by Faithlab., Macon GA,
www.faithlab.com.

ISBN 978-0-9839863-9-3

for

Meggie
A cherished voice in my life;
A passionate voice in the world.

&

Dan
Whose life of love and unselfish giving was shortened
by unexpected tragedy, but whose love of life will be
forever remembered.

Acknowledgements

We first find our language by listening to others. I can't remember the first words I formed, but I'm sure they mimicked the voice of my mom or dad. In subsequent years, I picked up the southern dialect of my geographic home, the colloquialisms of my immediate culture, the vocabulary of my academic areas and of course the faith language of my religious community. I've been finding my voice for years.

We never stop learning to speak. As I lived with the content of this book and worked to put it on paper, I meandered in and out of the presence of some wonderful persons. Each of them added a piece of vocabulary or a particular vocal tone to the finished product.

Mary Bates serves as the librarian at the Margaret Tiebel Memorial Library, in Eudora, Arkansas. I wandered into the library — a stranger to her — and she welcomed a strange writer into her space. After introducing myself and explaining the direction of my work, she simply asked what I needed. My only requests were a chair, a table large enough to hold a couple of books, my laptop, and access to electricity. All were provided. In fact, as the steady stream of people flowed in and out of the small building each day, she was just as welcoming and just as attentive to each of them as she was to me. It is my desire that the receptive spirit she conveys in her work each day is somehow reflected in these pages. I want you to be at home in these paragraphs. I hope the words provide something you need.

Mary Bates has a two-year-old niece named AriYana. AriYana came to the library one day while I was writing. She had all the curiosity, rambunctiousness and friendliness of an average child her age. But her intelligence and desire 'to know' far exceeded many children I've encountered. Much to the chagrin of her working aunt, she continually made her way to my workstation and risked reprimand with each venture. I assured Mary that AriYana was not disturbing me and asked if I could hold her and read her a book. Permission was given, and then I remembered (as a father of three grown daughters) that you never read just one book to a two-year-old. AriYana was just the reprieve I needed from the hours of thinking and typing. We made our way along the shelves — multiple times — and then made our way through the colorful pages of ten? Twelve? Twenty books? Time with AriYana created a space for smiles, wonder, learning and rest. Again, I'm trusting that her wonder, curiosity and sheer enjoyment of life have somehow slipped between these lines.

Johnette Wesley Crockett was my fifth grade elementary school teacher. I've never had a teacher who taught or loved me as well. I visited her during the writing of this work. While having communicated by telephone once or twice, I had not seen her in over thirty years. During the writing of this work, we spent an afternoon in her living room and remembered people and events together. She could name almost every student she had taught. Beyond that, she remembered their learning style and the unique ways she would alter classroom method and content to accommodate their needs and give them the best chance at success. She is a great observer of people — not just because she has the ability, but because she has a compassion that compels her to see. She stood on her porch in tears as I drove away. I hope I've reflected her insight and compassion in these paragraphs. It would honor me to honor her.

University Baptist Church in Hattiesburg, Mississippi has become somewhat of a laboratory for me. Pastor Rusty Edwards, Associate Pastor Ashley Gill, and all the laity that fill the pews are far from lab specimens, however! They are some of the best people I know. The substantive words contained in this manuscript passed by their listening ears before they were ever typed onto the screen of my computer. They nodded in approval or winced in puzzlement as I laid the ponderings of my heart before them. My thoughts were always treated as sacred gifts — even if contrary to their own. We spent as much time conversing as we did listening to my presentations. Their annual bible study and retreat sessions were moments of mutual benefit for us. This book was shaped there. As you read, I hope you're also able to hold sacred what I share. You need not agree with all of it or any of it. I promise I'll hold your side of the conversation sacred as well.

Whom do I acknowledge after praising the members of a Mississippi church? Well, the employees of a Mississippi casino of course! A huge thank you goes out to the staff of Harlow's Casino and Resort in Greenville, Mississippi. Greenville is across the Mississippi River from Eudora, Arkansas — about twenty miles. Harlow's is where I let my mind and body rest each evening during the writing of this manuscript. The rooms were clean and comfortable, the cards were dealt with fairness, and I have honestly never experienced a more genuinely friendly, courteous and helpful staff at any other hotel. From desk clerks to dealers, they are the best. If the tone of this book is any less friendly, I've not spoken or written well.

Outside the ArkLaMiss (what we natives call the tri-state region of Arkansas, Mississippi and Louisiana), my continued gratitude is extended to those who've helped me edit and publish this manuscript. David Cassady — my business partner — has been a patient driving force behind the work. David understood (on some days better than others) the nature of this book; it's not a product, it's my baby, and it took a little longer than prior projects to complete. This book is not just the dissemination of information. These words speak my heart's true faith. Joy Yee pored over each paragraph to insure a high standard of integrity, vulnerability, and consistency in my thought. Terry Cantwell helped clean up the grammar. Jean Trotter took a rough manuscript and worked her magic to make the final product attractive both inside and out.

I would be remiss if I did not mention the excellent baristas at the Barnes & Noble Coffee Shop in Macon, Georgia: Brande, Zac, AJ, Caylan, Chevelle, Ingrid, LaQuisha, Whitney and Katy Bug. As always, they kept the drinks flowing while I hammered away at the final form.

And finally, a deep word of gratitude goes to my family. I've been surrounded by kith and kin tolerating to differing degrees my need to explore the edges of faith and then take the time — often time away from them — to write about it. My extended family includes the good people of Northside Baptist Church in Eudora, Arkansas. Some seat themselves in that sanctuary of worship each Sunday and others now only reside in our memories. They have played an integral part in my faith development and in the formation of this book. They have gifted me in ways that may never be known or measured. They are my family.

Contents

Foreword

Faith is a dynamic thing. How do you put static words onto an experience that becomes a journey of stretching, growing, discovering, relating and becoming?

This book attempts to help us talk about God and faith in language that is accessible, authentic, and credible. It is not language that is meant to substitute for previous words about faith or to be exhaustive in scope. Throughout history, language has helped us to articulate what we understand about God. But all language also limits because God is infinitely greater than any combination of finite words that seek to explain, describe, teach, and give witness. If anything, this book adds a dimension of needed richness to language that has already been used to talk about scripture, humanity, salvation, God, Jesus, Holy Spirit, church, and the world.

In some ways, this is a language for moderate Christians to share what they believe with an extremely conservative audience, OR an audience that is not familiar with faith. Some of us are not comfortable with bumper sticker theology or faith that is easily explicable with sound bites. We tend to speak of our faith in paragraphs because we grapple with nuances and hard questions that invite us to enter gray areas where God remains a mystery.

In other ways this is a personal testimony. It is entirely appropriate that the author shares this "new" language as part of the personal story of his journey of faith, and the finding of his own voice. As such, his words remain true to what all faith statements are — simply a witness offered to others as a gift for them to consider in their own lives.

Whether you come to these words for the first time, or with a background of existing words that have framed your own faith, perhaps you will consider what deepened understandings might be offered to you as gifts within these pages.

Joy Yee, Pastor
Nineteenth Avenue Baptist Church
San Francisco, California
April, 2013

Introduction

Everything seems frozen in time. Well, almost everything. The little brick church with the white cinder block fellowship hall seems smaller and worn. A different name follows the word 'Pastor' on the little church sign. The field beside the church is now paved. Worn white lines create more spaces than are needed for the smattering of cars and trucks assembled there. I miss the grass that now lies dead beneath the asphalt. This was where I hunted Easter eggs, felt the exhilaration of pushing the accelerator and turning the steering wheel of a red 1969 Chevy pickup truck for the first time, and wiped sweat while pushing a lawnmower to do my service to God. To my adult eyes everything seems smaller. So do the homes that line the streets around it. The streets are narrower than I remember and each block of property seems compressed. But everything else is frozen in time.

I push open the door to the sanctuary of Northside Baptist Church. To the right — in what might be deemed a vestibule, but is decorated more like a home hallway — is the pastor's study. An old metal sign still says so. The door is locked, but I'm guessing the shelves are now filled with books the new pastor likes to read or look at. I'll bet it still smells as musty as it did when Brother Ready studied there.

A double door entry leads me into the sanctuary. I stop and count. Yep, still 28 pews. As a child I used to count one side then multiply times two as my family made its way to the second pew from the front on the preacher's left. It was our pew.

That pew was a second home for me. I slept, ate, sang, learned, played, laughed, and got whippings there. Yes, whippings. My antics were innocent, but disruptive. During the pastor's sermons, I would often open my Bible to the Song of Songs, lay the Bible in my younger brother's lap and point to a verse which contained the word 'breast.' He would not be able to contain himself and his snickers would earn him the first whipping. Mine would soon follow. During evening services, congregants were often invited to request hymns. Regardless of the season, I would inevitably thrust my hand into the air and request "What Child Is This?" or "Good Christian Men Rejoice." Both songs contained the word 'ass.'

As soon as the word left the mouths of the singing congregants, my younger brother would get whipped for laughing. Then I would get it. When I wasn't perusing the hymnal and Bible for cheap adolescent entertainment, I was attentively following the sermonic thought of my pastor, Brother Ready. I would tenaciously take notes on each of his sermons and dream of preaching the same gospel one day.

The present pastor has a pleasant demeanor and a delightful grin to match. He seems to be a genuine man who fills the role of pastor well. He also uses reading glasses that at the moment he has misplaced. Scanning the congregation of about twenty worshippers, he asks if anyone has seen them. Silence. Rather spontaneously, I offer him mine. He receives them with a smile, slides them along his temples over his ears, rests them at the end of his nose just above the grin and proceeds to lead us in worship. He reads scripture and delivers a sermon through my lenses. These are the slivers of glass through which I read and interpret scripture and through which I observe and engage the world. Even with the same lenses, we see things differently.

There is little difference between his sermon and the sermons I heard as a child, which were primarily gentle in tone. However, decibel levels were raised when the cross, hell, the devil or the world were mentioned. The faithful twenty who are gathered on this rainy Sunday evening are admonished to submit to God 100%. If we feel we've given any less, we are encouraged to kneel at the altar and pray for the ability to give more. I look around the room. Twenty memories. Twenty people who had been my Sunday School teachers, choir leaders, discipleship directors, surrogate parents, grandparents, and friends. Twenty citizens of an impoverished delta community and a church that by some people's standards has seen better days. Twenty people. I'm glad none of them go to the altar to pray.

While I also do not go to the altar to confess any of my shortcomings or fractional lack of commitment, I will confess here that I wonder. I wonder if these folk would really love me if they knew me. If they knew the lessons I had learned in this place had been renewed, reformed, and in some instances replaced by subsequent lessons along the way. My life has felt anything but frozen in time. The inspired but insulated faith of my childhood has been shaped and at times scarred by education, spirituality programs, the joys and struggles of marriage and parenting, poker tables, travels, brushes with other cultures and other denominations and other geographic regions, ironman training and a multitude of other life experiences in between. And maybe I've presumed too much about them! Maybe their thoughts and experiences have led them to a much broader and deeper understanding of God than I've relegated to my memory. Maybe, like me, they have felt and thought things they have hesitated to speak in church, speak in the coffee shop, or speak to one another, because it seems contrary to the common vernacular of their faith. I wonder how they will feel about the words of this book.

Following the service, we stand in the aisle of the church. We tell stories, share phone numbers, ask questions, laugh hard and allow ourselves to trickle a few tears. We hold common amazement at how much we love one another — the aging congregation and the prodigal preacher boy who has come home.

What am I doing here, I wonder? I've spent the last three days presenting the substance of this book during a conference at the University Baptist Church in Hattiesburg, Mississippi. Finding myself only a few hours from my childhood home — a place I had not seen in more than three decades — I decided to drive up and the see the town. Now that I'm here, it suddenly seems important to stay a while.

Scripture

I've decided to write the bulk of this manuscript at the Margaret Tiebel Memorial Library in Eudora, Arkansas. This library was my second home during the years I lived in Eudora and an easy bike ride away from where I lived. Almost every afternoon, I'd check the air in the tires of my gold Spyder bike (banana seat with high handlebars), throw a pack of saltines and my school books in the wire basket affixed to the front of my bike, and ride to the library. Homework was done as quickly as possible and then shelves were perused with my library friends, Kenneth and Cheryl. We'd turn in books from days before and take our newly borrowed books to the swing set outside. No sound but the rhythmic squeaking of chains and the munching of shared saltines could be heard as we buried ourselves in the books.

The swings are gone but the books are still here. As I type these words, I'm less than twenty feet from the favorite pages of my childhood: *Henry Huggins*, *Ellen Tebbits*, *The Sign in the Crooked Arrow* (the best

Hardy Boys book ever), *The Mystery of the Green Ghost* (the best Alfred Hitchcock and the Three Investigators book ever), *The Ghost of Windy Hill,* and *The Incredible Journey.* They are all still here, neatly shelved in alphabetical order ready for another child who wants to be swept away.

No book, however, delighted me more than the Bible. I memorized Bible verses the way some kids collected baseball cards. I read books about the Bible. I memorized the books of the Bible. I kept notebooks and journals of sermons and thoughts that our pastor shared about the Bible. I made sure to read something in the Bible every day. I'll admit it. I was (am) a Bible nerd.

Now here's where it gets weird. It wasn't just the content that drew me. It was also the tactile nature of this sacred book. Most books were limited to a hardback or paperback presentation. Not the Bible. My dad's Bible had a soft, black, leather cover with the very thinnest of interior pages. They almost felt like the 'onion skin paper' we used for tracing in school. The Good News Version of the Bible was paperback with a newsprint feel. The Living Bible had a green padded cover. Every Bible had a different feel and texture. I loved the variety of wrappings that held the sacred word.

Cheatham's Drugstore is where Bibles were purchased in Eudora. On the corner of Main Street, in the center of town, the drug store doors opened to a display of Bibles, front and center in the entryway. Every Bible I owned as a child was purchased at the drugstore. And the one Bible I wanted was prominently displayed, but economically out of reach. I already owned a small red gift Bible and a red *Youth for Christ* Bible, complete with a forward by Billy Graham. The former was presented to me by Mrs. Cheatham upon entering the Primary Department of our Sunday School. The latter was presented to me by Mrs. Cheatham when I surrendered to preach. Because the Cheathams owned the drugstore, they presented a lot of Bibles. The one Bible I wanted, however, was a Thompson Chain Reference Study Bible. It was the Bible from which my pastor, Brother Ready, preached.

Six years after moving from Eudora, I was ordained to the gospel ministry at Parkwood Hills Baptist Church in Decatur, Georgia. At the conclusion of the ordination service, the church presented me with a leather-bound Thompson Chain Reference

Study Bible that I received with great gratitude and excitement. A large part of me wished Mrs. Cheatham had been there to present it to me.

I now have a shelf full of Bibles. Each is filled with the same story, and yet each has its own story too. Some were gifted by caring individuals. Others were purchased for a particular purpose. A few are sacred souvenirs of holy places and moments in my past. Each and every one has contributed to my life's journey.

For me, the scripture has provided the beginnings of conversations with God, not the end.

My red *Youth for Christ* Bible bears the marks of a faithful teenager's enthusiasm. The cover is worn, predictable verses are underlined or highlighted, favorite sermon quotes are penciled on the blank pages near the cover, and a couple of stickers adorn the exterior. One of those stickers reads, "The Bible says it, I believe it, that settles it." I've heard it said there's nothing more dangerous than a zealous teenager with a Bible!

My earliest view of scripture assumed that the words of holy text were given in order to establish belief. Within the sixty-six books of my Bible were the answers to every question and the direction for every path. My ability to identify these 'answers' and rightly discern these paths was greatly influenced by the most charismatic religious figures in my life. Almost any teacher, preacher, or youth minister that was forceful in their demeanor or entertaining in their approach could draw me in. I was hungry to know and they knew it.

In my young mind, I couldn't imagine there could be any disagreement over the truth of scripture, particularly as I had learned it and begun to dispense it. It all made sense to me — just as it had been explained to me. As long as I stayed within the parameters of the beliefs delivered to me, the parameters of my limited faith community and the parameters of a fairly untainted life, my understanding of the Bible was more than sufficient. However, when issues outside my limited theological thought were introduced to me in seminary or when I ran head on into an Episcopalian or a Pentecostal or — God forbid — a Jewish person, or when life dealt my parents a divorce, one of my children an addiction, or one of my friends a brain tumor, my certainties about verses were brutally transformed into argumentative prayers. It was at each of these points my relationship with scripture expanded and I was able to consider approaches to text that differed from that with which I was raised. While foreign to me, the idea of arguing with scripture and praying with scripture had long been part of faith tradition. Within the Jewish tradition, faith is shaped and understood through the aggressive engagement of ideas and arguments. In the history of the church, the sacred reading of scripture was considered a valid avenue of truth — particularly among the saints. In our own era of modern enlightenment, the historical understanding of biblical backgrounds has provided novel, needed, and meaningful insights into the biblical writings.

The assertion 'the Bible says it and I believe it' was starting to settle very little if anything. I was beginning to suspect that the Bible was never meant to be a guide for dogma. What if it was not meant to contain the answers that end all arguments? What if the words of scripture were the beginnings of our conversations with God, not the end? What if the Bible is where our arguments with God start instead? Where the path is negotiated, not necessarily revealed. These questions were troubling at times, but troubling breaths of fresh air. They were filled with life and allowed God to become bigger and bigger and bigger.

I've always been a bit partial to the Book of Leviticus. I'm aware that most Christians fall in love with the psalms, one of the gospels, or a Pauline letter. But I've always been drawn to the corpus of priestly law contained in this oft-neglected book. It is indeed a long and laborious listing of the rituals and rules that dictate the worship and work of the Israelite community. However, nestled within the listing of legal matters is a single narrative. In Leviticus 10, we read the story of the death of two of Aaron's sons, Nadab and Abihu. It's actually more than a mere death. They are killed by a God who seems capricious.

According to the text, Aaron's sons are participating in the burning of a sacrificial offering to God. The details of their infraction is unclear, but they do something wrong in the process and the law is not followed. God immediately strikes them dead. After all, the law is clear. There is a prior verse in Leviticus that states exactly how the offering is to be presented to God. They did not give that particular verse adequate attention and God struck them dead. Now, if we ended the story here, the lesson would be simple — the Bible says it, you better believe it, and that settles it. Do exactly what every verse says or risk a heavenly whammy! This is not the end of the story, however. And it's in the subsequent scene that the role of scripture is more broadly defined for us and questions arise.

Moses summons Aaron after Aaron's sons are killed. Entering the sacrificial scene that is complete with dead animals and dead sons, Moses instructs Aaron to complete the sacrifice. With regard to this particular sacrifice, Aaron is to take a portion of the offering home and enjoy a feast with family and friends. This is the law. There is a verse that says this must be done. And we've already seen what happens when the law is not obeyed! Aaron, however, looks at Moses and basically exclaims, "Are you crazy?!? I've got two dead sons on the floor! I am not going to eat a celebrative feast before God on the day that two of my sons have died!" (My personal translation of the text.) To make sure he is not consumed by the extraneous heat of impending lightning, Moses should be ducking. No lightning comes, however. Moses agrees with Aaron and Aaron departs to bury his sons. The message of the story seems to be two-fold. We should always take the text seriously, but it also demands a conversation — sometimes an argument.

This was Jesus' way. When confronted with verses about Sabbath, lepers or adulterous persons, there was obvious, prayerful conversation between Jesus and his Father, as well as between Jesus and those around him.

These kinds of conversations are not new for us. We've had these conversations around many issues and we've avoided them with regard to other issues. Few of us destroy our homes when mold is found in a closet or bathroom. According to Levitical law, a single occurrence of mold compels us to scrape down the walls of our homes. A reoccurrence, however, demands the destruction of our homes! Few of us would destroy where we live when mold is found in a closet or bathroom. I've met no one who stones their children to death for disrespectful behavior or stones their neighbor for ignoring the Sabbath. Most of us wear clothing of blended fabric and don't think twice about eating a cheeseburger — both breaches of God's law. Oh yes, there is a verse in the Bible that says these things cannot be done! But we do them, I assume, because we have had some sort of conversation with God. Maybe it was a formal prayer or maybe it was in the recesses of our mind, but the conversation was engaged just the same. A better understanding of biological and social sciences, as well as, a more personal understanding of God, through Jesus, has allowed us to approach these verses differently. We converse with them and about them. We argue. We respect them, but often relinquish the dominant hold they have had on our lives and the lives of those before us.

However, there are conversations regarding other subjects or laws that we avoid or ignore. Christians continue to pick and choose levitical laws to 'hold onto' for the express purpose of condemning others. We are willing to have conversations about the laws we feel might impede our lives and faith, but stringently obligate others to laws that address areas of life that do not pose any particular struggle for us. We act as if some laws are non-negotiable. I would suggest that all laws — in fact, all biblical texts — are the beginning of the conversation, not the end. If there is no ongoing conversation and the verses are eternal 'rules of law,' then there is no need for God's voice. There is no need for prayer, study or even discussion. It has already been said. There is nothing more to say. But, in fact, there is more to be said. Words often need to be argued with in order to be understood. These conversations are essential to our maturity and faith development.

The scriptures also provide a continued path for faith development and maturity.

Lest I sound too brutal with regard to the simple, dogmatic reading of the text with which I grew up, it is part of the path. It is not, however, the end of the path. Sunday school teachers who taught me to read the text as a concrete document where everything was black and white or right and wrong were giving me exactly what I needed at the time. It was age appropriate for a child in the faith. I was where I needed to be at the time, but I didn't need to stay there!

The Apostle Paul hints at this numerous times in his writings. Writing to the church at Corinth he comments, "When I was a child, I thought like a child. But when I became an adult, I put away childish things." He encouraged the Corinthians to move beyond the 'milk of the gospel' and consume the 'meat of faith.' He told the church in Galatia the law was nothing more than a babysitter for us — a nanny — until we reached maturity in Christ.

The law — the dogmatic, simple reading of scripture — is a part of our faith journey. But it shouldn't be the end.

In Jewish faith, the Hebrew Scriptures are the source for faith development. Their order intentionally aids this process. Christianity's embrace of the Hebrew Scriptures was a natural and wonderful decision. But, rather than transfer the Hebrew Scriptures to our Bible in their traditional order, we rearranged and re-categorized the books. The Hebrew Scriptures are divided into three sections: Law, Prophets and Writings. The books of law are identical to the Protestant Old Testament's books of law: Genesis, Exodus, Leviticus, Numbers, and Deuteronomy. The differences in order and category come with the books that follow. The Hebrew Prophets include most of what we categorize as history in addition to the prophetic books: Joshua, Judges, 1 & 2 Samuel, 1 & 2 Kings, and all of the Protestant Scripture's traditional prophets (major and minor) except for Daniel and Lamentations. The third section of the Hebrew Scriptures (the Writings) includes what we typically categorize as poetry (Psalms, Proverbs, Job, Ecclesiastes, Song of Songs) along with some historical books and prophetic writings (Ruth, Esther,

Ezra, Nehemiah, 1 & 2 Chronicles, Daniel, and
Lamentations). If you're trying to get this straight in
your head, don't think too hard. My only purpose is
to highlight Christianity's loss in the rearrangement
of these materials.

HEBREW CANON		PROTESTANT CANON	
TORAH	Genesis Exodus Leviticus Numbers Deuteronomy	Genesis Exodus Leviticus Numbers Deuteronomy	LAW (Pentateuch)
PROPHETS	Joshua Judges I Samuel II Samuel I Kings II Kings Isaiah Jeremiah Exekiel Hosea Joel Amos Obadiah Jonah Micah Nahum Habakkuk Zephaniah Haggai Zechariah Malachi	Joshua Judges Ruth I Samuel II Samuel I Kings II Kings I Chronicles II Chronicles Ezra Nehemiah Esther	HISTORY
		Psalms Job Proverbs Ecclesiastes Song of Solomon	POETRY and WISDOM
		Isaiah Jeremiah Lamentations Exekiel Daniel	MAJOR PROPHETS
THE WRITINGS	Psalms Job Proverbs Ruth Song of Solomon Ecclesiastes Lamentations Esther Daniel Ezra Nehemiah I Chronicles II Chronicles	Hosea Joel Amos Obadiah Jonah Micah Nahum Habakkuk Zephaniah Haggai Zechariah Malachi	MINOR PROPHETS

The simplest argument for our shift in the order of Hebrew Scriptures is that the Christian readers arranged the books by 'style' of literature. As previously stated, this was not the criteria for the Jewish arrangement of the books. The Hebrew Scriptures are categorized in the order of their authority, the order of their compilation, and most importantly, the order of their usage in faith development. It is the latter that is of greatest interest to us.

In Jewish faith development, the Law is the starting point. Prior to present day Bar and Bat Mitzvahs, children engage the primary stories of the faith contained in Genesis to Deuteronomy, as well as, the traditional 613 mitzvot or commandments couched in these chapters and verses. It is only after the learning of law — the black and white basics of the faith — that the Prophets are studied. The prophetic literature argues and struggles with the law. Like teenagers questioning the hard and fast rules of their parents, the prophets hammered at and honed the requirements of the law. For instance, in Deuteronomy 23:1-5, the law makes it very clear that no eunuch or Moabite is allowed entrance into the faith community of Israel. This is the law — black and white, right and wrong. However, in Isaiah 56:3-7, the prophet argues that eunuchs and foreigners are welcomed into God's house — a house of prayer for all people — if they choose to keep Sabbath and hold fast to God's covenant. Then Isaiah, writing from Babylonian exile amid a population of foreigners, has no doubt lived long enough to know that all foreigners aren't bad. There are some really good Moabites and Babylonians outside the faith and some bad ones. Just like there are some good people 'inside' the faith and some bad ones. In Isaiah's mind and writings, the law simply can't be the last word. It is a part of faith development. It is the first step of faith development but not the last. And by the time we get to the Writings section of the Hebrew Scriptures, we read the story of Ruth. Ruth is a Moabite who marries an Israelite and becomes the great grandmother of King David!

By moving Ruth to an historical division of the Christian Scriptures (making Ruth the eighth book of our Old Testament rather than one of the concluding books of the whole corpus of scripture), we lose the significant movement of faith development: no Moabites (the Law), let a good Moabite in the community of faith (the Prophets), marry a Moabite and make them part of the family (the Writings).

This does not mean that the law is ignored. It means that the law has become the backdrop for all decision-making, but is not allowed to be static and oppressive as faith develops in healthy, sensible, and sacred ways.

I have three daughters. When they were pre-schoolers, I stood them all in front of our stove and said (with as much authority as I could muster), "Don't ever, ever, ever, ever touch this stove. It is hot. It will burn you. It will hurt." "Remember," I reiterated and emphasized and exclaimed, "Don't ever touch this stove."

A few years later, when my middle school daughters sought to interrupt my 'television time' with a request for frozen pizza, I told them to carefully pre-heat the oven, use oven mitts to place the pizza on the middle rack, and when the timer beeped use the mitts to carefully remove the pizza. I must admit, I even dragged myself off the sofa the first couple of times to make sure they were careful.

Today? My daughters are in their mid-twenties. When they come home to visit, I expect them to cook supper! I want them to interact with the stove! This does not mean that my first words to them concerning the stove were meaningless, false, or meant to be forgotten. They will forever handle the stove with the 'law' in the back of their mind. They will forever know that the stove has the capacity to hurt or burn them. They also know, however, that dealing with a stove is part of living as a mature adult. The law is a backdrop for living well with the stove. It was never meant…let me say that again…NEVER MEANT to impede usage of the stove for all time. It was NEVER MEANT to be a rule that oppressed or limited their adult lives. To use the Apostle Paul's idea, the law was a babysitter — a nanny — until my daughters were old enough and mature enough to live well in the presence of a stove.

The original order of the Hebrew Scriptures allows us to see this process of faith development and affords us a healthy movement from to law to life. The law prepares us for the struggle inherent in dealing with Moabites — the ever present other. But life is filled with meaningful and marvelous stories of encounters and relationships with the other — Ruth. The Law tells us that food and sexuality and suffering will challenge our primary love for God. But the Writings — Ecclesiastes and Song of Songs and Job — assure us that these same issues are a part of the rich fabric of life.

This faith development is vividly evident in the life of Jesus. Jesus knew the law concerning Sabbath observance. He argued with the Pharisees about the meaning of those laws. And finally, he lived what seemed to be contrary to the law when he healed on the Sabbath. Jesus knew the law concerning the treatment of lepers — banishment and quarantine. But Jesus touched and loved and healed lepers. Jesus was not disregarding law. The law was always the backdrop from which Jesus made his life decisions. Jesus did not, however, allow the law to dictate his life when life demanded a more graceful path.

The scriptures then are the beginning of a conversation with God that allows for the wonderful process of faith development. Of course, most of our maturing was not guided by a single voice or perspective. Most of us have had numerous teachers, mentors, and guides who prompted us to explore and experience life from multiple perspectives. The same is true with scripture.

The scriptures provide multiple voices that must be heard.

When I hear people argue about religious matters, they typically defend their view from one of four perspectives: relationship, power, morality, or ritual. Any argument within the life of the church can usually be reduced to the questions of: whose feelings will be hurt (relationship), how will the direction of the church be set (power), what is considered right or wrong (moral), and how does this compare to how we've done it in the past (ritual)?

I was privileged to serve almost fifteen years in my last pastorate. During those fifteen years our congregation held discussions concerning: the role of women in the life of the church, the placement of the national flag in the sanctuary, the presence of and openness to gays and lesbians in the church, the form of baptism, the establishment of a columbarium, and numerous other issues. In each of these discussions, persons tended to posture themselves according to one of the four aforementioned perspectives. And, in most cases, they argued every issue from that particular perspective.

There are a few things you learn in seminary that you wonder if you will ever need or use. They don't fit comfortably into first-year-seminarian sermon outlines, and thus, it is assumed they will never fit into a sermon outline. What use then is such information?!? Such is the case with Source Criticism of the Old Testament. It's a discipline that simply asks, "Who wrote this material?"

During an Introduction to Old Testament class, I was introduced to the legendary JEDP. At the risk of having some professor somewhere revoke my seminary degree and require me to matriculate, study, and earn my degrees all over again, I am going to admittedly reduce this wonderful concept to manageable terms and parameters. So, in a proverbial nutshell, four different voices tell the story we find in the Old Testament. These unique perspectives are identified by scholars as: the Jahwist (J), the Elohist (E), the Deuteronomist (D) and the Priestly writer (P). These are not individuals that produced particular passages of scripture, but rather communities or pockets of people who held a particular point of view. While certain voices dominate certain books (i.e. the Deuteronomist is responsible for the whole of Deuteronomy and the Priestly writer provides the vast majority of material for the book of Leviticus), these four voices are edited, overlapped, and intermingled in the books of Genesis, Exodus, and Numbers. Later, the prophets will respond to each of these voices — at times identifying with them and at other times challenging them. Like us, prophets tend to gravitate toward and find one voice or one perspective more comfortable than another. In doing so, they tend to speak from a particular voice and thus seem critical or even dismissive of the others.

The Jahwist voice is primarily interested in relationship. It views faith as a personal, covenanted relationship between God and humankind. It is concerned with genuine intimacy with God and one another. It is most easily identified in our translations of the Old Testament when God is referred to as 'Lord God.' The use of the word 'Lord' indicates the presence of the personal name of God in the Hebrew text. The use of this name denotes the writer's tendency toward a more casual familiarity with God — a personal, comfortable, loving relationship that allows the use of the sacred, personal name, Yahweh. Of the two creation stories presented in Genesis 1 and 2, Genesis 2 is a product of the Jahwist voice. The 'Lord God' reaches down and forms man from the dust of the earth, breathes the breath of life into his nostrils, cares about his loneliness, reaches into his side to remove a rib and fashions a companion. This personification of God is very 'touch oriented' and lovingly relational in its presentation.

The Elohist is most often contrasted with the Jahwist. While the Jahwist is more concerned with relationship and to some degree individuality, the Elohist is concerned with power and the movement of the community. Some scholars trace the political slant of these voices to the beginnings of the Divided Monarchy in Israel. After the death of David's son, Solomon, the monarchy became a divided kingdom. The Southern Kingdom (Judah) was ruled by Rehoboam — the son of Solomon. Rehoboam was appointed king on the basis of relationship. The Southern Kingdom continued to follow an hereditary monarchy. The Northern Kingdom (Israel) was ruled by Jeroboam — a former military leader under King Solomon. Jeroboam was a symbol of charismatic power. He rallied the people to disassociate themselves from the nepotistic rule of the royal family of Jerusalem, the capital of the Southern Kingdom. They chose to reorder governance according to their interpretation of Mosaic law with little or no regard for the relational entitlement claimed by the off-spring of David. They chose to follow the practice of an elected monarchy. They believed that God could act powerfully through any chosen person. God is always referred to as 'God' (Elohim) in Elohist materials, never "Lord God.' And usually, the powerful acts of God performed in the books of Genesis and Exodus are a product of the pen of the Elohist.

The Deuteronomist writes from the predominant perspective of morality. God is not exclusively relational, powerful, or ritualistic. Rather, God is portrayed as demanding particular behavior by rewarding those who obey and punishing those who disobey. The Book of Deuteronomy (*deutero* — second, *nomos* — law) repeats the story of the Exodus in an abbreviated, sermonic form and then restates the laws given at Sinai. This rendering, however, includes predictable curses and punishments for those who disobey! Subsequent biblical books — Joshua, Judges, 1 Samuel, 2 Samuel, 1 Kings, and 2 Kings — convey the perspective of the Deuteronomist as well. Each of these books recount Israel's story as a cycle of: obedience then failure then punishment then forgiveness then obedience then failure then punishment then forgiveness — over and over again.

Moral behavior, not relationship or power or ritual, dictates how God relates to us.

Going back to the creation narratives of Genesis 1 and 2, we find the first appearance of the Priestly voice in Genesis 1. The Priestly voice contends that relationship to God is shaped by order and ritual. God is a transcendent God rather than a close, intimate God. God must be properly approached and properly addressed. The Priestly voice of Genesis 1 contains more formulaic language, only uses the formal name of God (Elohim and never Yahweh) and actually contains a hint of priestly ritual — Sabbath observance. The orderly nature of creation in Genesis 1 is reflective of the orderly nature of life presented in the laws of Leviticus — a larger corpus produced by the priestly voice. The chapter ends with God observing Sabbath — a priestly ordering of time that is not commanded until the law is given at Sinai in Exodus 20. These hints of sacrifice, priestly roles and the sacredness of time will appear several times before the law is ever given in Exodus and Leviticus. The Priestly writer is intent upon showing and arguing early documentation and validation of sacred ritual.

All of these stories in our Old Testament literature were probably edited and compiled while

Israel was exiled in Babylon from 586 BCE to 539 BCE. After decades of living in the Promised Land under a united and later divided monarchy, Israel was completely overrun by the Babylonians. During their enslavement in Babylon, it became necessary to retain their language and history, as well as, thoughtfully ask the obvious questions: "Why are we in exile? Where is God? Will we ever be free again?" The writing of the Hebrew scriptures addressed both concerns. These written stories allowed for the retention of language, heritage, and history. The content of the stories addressed the concerns of the enslaved Hebrews. Of course, not all Hebrews could agree on the answers to these questions. For the Jahwist, God's loving faithfulness to Israel would prompt God's continued care and eventual deliverance. For the Elohist, hope was centered on God's past provision of charismatic, powerful military leaders to defeat the enemies at hand. For the Deuteronomist, enslavement was a result of moral indiscretions. Repentance was necessary for the exile to end. For the Priestly writer, a restoration of temple ritual would restore Israel's place in the world and the heart of God. As a slave in Babylon, one could read the stories of Genesis, Exodus, Leviticus, Numbers, Deuteronomy and later texts, and find multiple voices providing hope and challenge for the future. And let's be honest, everyone wasn't enslaved for the same reason and everyone didn't find hope in the same place. At their best, the scriptures are a written witness to the human experience of God. And people tend to experience God in all sorts of valid, different ways.

One of the mysterious beauties of the biblical text (and quite frankly, one of the miraculous methods of the biblical editors) is the inclusion of all these multiple, divergent voices and perspectives. We are a human population of diverse personalities. As individuals and even congregations, we relate to God differently. Our life circumstances are extremely varied. The inclusion of multiple voices in biblical text makes it relevant and readable for all of us. If the editors of biblical text had left any perspective out, or if God had chosen to only speak in one dialect, how would we have all heard? The miracle of Pentecost in Acts 2 is truly the miracle of scripture, "How is it that each of us hears in our native language?" The scriptures provide multiple voices that must be heard.

Some of us worship and relate to a very transcendent God. We are comfortable with a sense of distance. We rely on ritual — the litanies and liturgies of our faith — to usher us into and assure us of God's presence. We easily hear the words of Genesis 1. Others among us feel very close to God. In the words of the hymn writer, "He walks with me and he talks with me. And He tells me I am His own." The imminence of God is very real and the voice of God is very close and familiar. These are Genesis 2 people. The multiple voices inherent in scripture allow each of us and all of us to find our sense of God.

During my years as a pastor, I often found myself in the home of a recently deceased individual I barely knew. Yet, I was called to speak final, sacred words on their life. On the eve of the funeral, family and friends would gather to speak with me. Each had stories to tell of their particular experiences with and impressions of the departed. The stories were often divergent; you would think they were speaking of different people. One adult child would sentimentally recall, "The sound of Mama's voice was like a cool clear drink of water on a hot day," while her siblings sat in a corner eyeing one another in disbelief — inconspicuously, ever so slightly, shaking their heads from side to side. As a minister, I listened to all of these voices as I pieced together the person whose life was primarily a mystery to me. The scriptures provide the same messy miracle with regard to the mystery of God.

Of course, these multiple voices also remind us how necessary diversity can be. The diversity of the text keeps God large and mysterious. The diversity calls us away from our favorite mentally graven images of God and invites us to see God through another set of lenses. The diversity of holy experience in biblical text validates the multiple voices in contemporary dialogue. I need to hear the conservative voice and the liberal voice. I need relational language and ritual language. I need to bounce my behavior off a moral barometer. All of these voices serve as a check and balance for my particular experience of God, both personally and within the parameters of my faith family.

So what is the ultimate purpose of this living, active document that is the beginning of a conversation with God, assembled for our faith development, and replete with so many voices and perspectives?

The scriptures provide a space for the Spirit of God to do the work of God in our lives.

It is in our conversation with God, our developing understanding of God, and the multiple perspectives of God that God is able to do God's work in us. I grew up understanding scripture as a static and stable text. The unchanging and unarguable nature of the text was repeatedly highlighted in sermon and lesson. Those who taught me seemed to believe that the answers of life were forthright and fixed within the biblical verses. In contrast, the ideas of conversation, faith development, and multiple voices present an approach to biblical text that is open and bursting with possibilities. Rather than reducing options and limiting God and life to a narrow understanding of law, a space is created where anything can happen. God is unlimited. An impoverished, widowed Moabite woman can find her way to a field in Bethlehem, marry an Israelite — even though the law forbids it — and become the great grandmother of King David, the great grandmother of Jesus!

An Ethiopian eunuch (Acts 8) — although forbidden by Israelite law — can be baptized and made part of the faith family. And today, others who have been excluded on the basis of 'a verse' in the Bible, can be included because of ongoing conversation, healthy faith development, and an open ear to multiple voices that all provide a space for God to do God's work in us. This is what keeps the scriptures 'living and active.' This open interchange between God and community and individual is what keeps the Bible from becoming a stagnant document that barely addresses the realities of each subsequent generation. "The Bible says it," we can engage it and possibly find ourselves encountering a God who is larger than we ever imagined.

Humanity

I received mixed messages as a child. The saints that surrounded me in my home church drew the best from me, hoped the best for me and gave me every opportunity to be what God might shape me to be.

I've always been able to carry a tune and I've spent most of my life carrying a guitar around. The good folk at church allowed and encouraged me to carry both in worship. The Dant children often gathered around the church piano as my sister, a budding southern gospel pianist, banged out the chord progressions and rhythms for our presentation of classics like: "Turn Your Radio On," "Jesus Is Coming Soon" and "I've Been Changed." In later years, I stood alone with a Sears Silvertone acoustic guitar and crooned my crossover tunes for the congregation. It was my favorite type of solo. I would choose a secular song that could be lyrically adjusted for church use. Mac Davis' "I Believe in Music" became "I Believe in Jesus" and Olivia Newton John's "Let Me Be There" became "Let Him Be There." These offerings from an eight- or ten- or thirteen-year-old were always received with applause and accolades.

As a seventh grader, I attended a youth camp in Siloam Springs, Arkansas. It was during this camp experience that I 'surrendered to preach.' In the same way the musical microphone was offered to me, the pulpit was shared. In the little Baptist churches of southern Arkansas, if you were 'called to preach' you were supposed to preach. It didn't matter if you were called at fifteen, fifty, or beyond. So, once a month on a Sunday evening, I was allowed to 'rightly divide the word of truth' for the gathered faithful. I'm not sure my division was so hot back then, but everyone seemed genuinely moved and graciously receptive of God's messy message from the golden child. That's what I felt like, a golden child…well, for at least half the time.

While on the one hand I seemed to be God's gift to those gathered on Archer Street, on the other hand, I was weekly reminded how sinful, depraved, and worthless I was. Sermons often reduced my life to filthy rags, hopeless battles, and the cause of a crucifixion.

I received mixed messages from the people around me — and in my formative mind — mixed messages from God. These somewhat contradictory communications led to a faith crisis not uncommon to those who were immersed in religious communities as children. We know we are loved. We know we are of value. But at the same time we carry a shame that makes us wonder if we are loved...really.

A few years ago, a couple came to my office for pastoral counseling. Although not stated, they had intimated some marital difficulties when making the appointment. Sitting on the ironically named 'love seat,' they mumbled through several moments of small talk. Finally, I asked, "Why are you here today?"

She spoke first. "He doesn't love me."

After what seemed like minutes, but I'm sure was only seconds, he looked at her and responded with a sense of pain and longing, "If you think that, you don't really know me and you obviously don't know who you are to me."

Who are you to God? Who am I to God? Who are we to God? As the Psalmist asked, "What are human beings that God is mindful of them?"

Humans are a reflection of God's image.

Every one of us (all 7 billion human beings on the face of this planet) bears a resemblance to God. We all have God's DNA flowing through our souls. If the Genesis text is accurate in its assessment of the human condition, then humankind was created in God's image. In God's image, male and female, God created humankind. There are no exceptions.

Years ago, I was asked to speak to a seminary preaching class about the art of the funeral sermon. I shared with the class my process for preparing a eulogy. I begin by reflecting on the life of the deceased and I ask, "What part of God's nature did I see in his or her life?" Every one of us has some part of the image of God in us. Every one of us! In fact, I've never met a person that didn't have a piece of God in him or her. I've had some close calls, but I've always been able to find some resemblance there!

Don was a scoundrel. I don't use that word very often, but I don't mind using it in reference to Don. He hunted out of season and begrudgingly paid the fines when caught. He cut trees on protected wetlands without the proper permits and begrudgingly paid those fines too. He cussed me in the church vestibule if any line of a sermon touched any corner of his conscience.

When Don became ill and was hospitalized in a nearby city, I told our congregation during a Wednesday evening prayer service I would come into the office for a few minutes the next morning and then travel to visit him. The next morning, I went into the office as planned. After completing my intended tasks, I hopped in my Honda Civic and buckled up for the ride to the hospital. Before starting the car, I noticed a brown paper bag had been placed in the passenger seat while I was working in the office. I opened the bag and pulled out a six-pack of Coors Light beer. A note was attached, "I heard you were going to visit Don and thought you might need these."

On the day of Don's funeral, his church family gathered and they sat on the edges of their seats waiting to see what part of the image of God I had seen in his life. They knew how I had brought this holy vision to the lives of numerous other members, but this was Don. And Don was a scoundrel. Many of them did not know I had buried one of Don's friends just months before. We had stood at the graveside of

Don's friend. As I spoke the final words of interment, Don cried.

As I began Don's eulogy, I opened my Bible to John 11:35 and read the two words printed there, "Jesus wept." I spoke for a moment about God's flow of tears for the Ninevites in the Book of Jonah. I talked about Jesus weeping over Jerusalem. I came full circle to the grave of Lazarus, one of Jesus' friends. We see Jesus crying there. I finally said, "Anyone who weeps over the death of friend has a piece of God in him." And we all wept for Don.

I have never met a human being who does not reflect the image of God. This is not an extremely difficult truth for us to embrace. We've heard it all our lives. And yet, if this notion from Genesis 1 is true, then I feel compelled to believe this assertion in Genesis 2 as well.

Humans are a reflection of God's limits.

Has there ever been a time in human history when God and man were any closer? It was just Adam and God in Eden. According to the story, there was no one else to garner God's attention in the garden. No one else had prayers to offer or problems to solve or joys to share. Every evening, in the cool of the evening, it was just the two of them. But, despite this personal proximity Adam enjoyed with his maker, God noted (Genesis 2:18) the man was lonely. In this one observation, God admitted God's limit. God cannot be everything for us. God cannot fulfill every human need and desire. God alone cannot curb loneliness. In fact, in Christian tradition, even God exists in community as the Trinitarian Father, Son, and Holy Spirit. Relationship, not loneliness, is the essence of God's existence.

I've often heard people assert that God is all they need. They claim that a relationship with the Son of God, Jesus, fulfills every longing of their existence. But as we've seen, a close reading of Genesis 2 asserts just the opposite. Even God recognized God's inability to appease our need for community.

So, God does what any good parent does when his or her child is in need of companionship. God offers Adam a pet. In the creation narrative of Genesis 2, God parades a host of animals before Adam. Adam names each one, but chooses none as a companion. It is only when God creates Eve that Adam announces his delight with one who is like him — bone of bone and flesh of flesh. Unlike the untouchable, invisible and predominantly silent God, this new creation can hold and be held, touch and be touched, speak and listen, and understand the human condition. And while we often hear this passage preached as the first marriage, it might better be understood as the first experience of human community and companionship — the elimination of loneliness.

God exists in community. God created a human that needed community. Each individual human reflects God's limits because God cannot fulfill all our needs. God knows we need each other.

From a burning bush, God called Moses to be God's instrument of Israel's deliverance from the Egyptians. We are all familiar with Moses' objections. He did not know God's name, did not think the people would believe he was God's messenger, and was concerned that he was unable to speak well. God responded to these objections with heavenly proclamations and miraculous signs. Neither God's words nor God's works were convincing. It was not until God offered to send Moses' brother Aaron with him that Moses finally responded, "Okay, I'll go." Aaron's presence tipped the scales. In the limits of our humanity, any struggle, challenge, or situation can be faced if one other human being 'gets us' and will go with us.

Linda was standing behind me in the supper line. I recently pastored a church that hosted a Wednesday Night Supper and Prayer Service each week. I turned to Linda as our green beans were being dipped and asked, "Did you hear about Kristen?"

"No," she replied. "Is she okay?"

I was hoping Linda had already heard. I took a deep breath and released the information, "She was diagnosed with breast cancer this past Monday."

I did not get another word out of my mouth before Linda responded, "I'd be happy to."

Without being asked, Linda knew I wanted her to talk to Kristen. Linda had received the same diagnosis over a year before. She had undergone numerous consultations, a series of curative and reconstructive surgeries, as well as, the accompanying treatments. She knew how important it was to have someone to walk with you — someone who understands...and gets you. She understood that in the challenges and struggles of life, we do not want to be alone. We need human community. God knows we need each other because we reflect God's admitted limits. And if all this is not amazing and graceful enough...

Humans are a reflection of God's good intentions.

The first story that follows the accounts of creation is the infamous temptation of Adam and Eve. Enter that sly slinky serpent who seems to know both the heart of humanity and the heart of God. The serpent entices the human to eat of the forbidden fruit with a two-fold argument — you'll know all you need to know and God's not really going to kill you. The serpent is truthful on both counts.

In eating the forbidden fruit, Adam and Eve learned what they needed to learn. Contrary to popular belief, this was not the first act of disobedience by humankind. Earlier, in Genesis 1:28, God's human creations had been instructed to '...be fruitful and multiply and fill the earth....' By chapter 3, there was still no multiplying going on! And rather than filling the earth, they seemed content just to hang out in the garden. It was only after the ingestion of forbidden fruit that humanity had the good sense to know that they were naked. And, in chapter 4, they got on with doing what naked people do. The serpent was right. They found what they needed to know.

The serpent was also correct in that God did not kill them. They did not 'surely die' on the day the fruit was eaten. Rather, we get a glimpse of God's grace, and better yet, God's intention with regard to his human creation. Following their fruitful feast, Adam and Eve heard God in the garden. They immediately hid. God asked them, "Where are you? Why are you hiding? Who told you that you were naked?" While each of the questions scraped at the evident guilt or shame being carried by Adam and Eve, it is the latter that captivates me — *"Who told you that you were naked?"*

Who told you that you were naked? Or said another way, who told you that there is something wrong with the way I created you? Who told you that you needed to be ashamed of the way I intended you to be?

We are uniquely created exactly the way God wants us to be. We are human. Not perfect. Not without flaw. Not without the capacity for all sorts of ungodly mischief, meanness, and messiness. But according to God, we are good. Very good! God intentionally created us to be human. As stated earlier, we each reflect the image of God and carry God's holy DNA. But, unlike God, we are not perfect and self-sufficient. We are human. And as hard as it may be to believe, that's exactly what God intended us to be. God loves us in our humanness.

That's right. You. Me. With all our quirky personalities, odd interests, deep passions, likes, dislikes, and preferences. We are exactly who God created us to be. In fact, I am absolutely convinced, most of the guilt and shame we carry doesn't come from God. It comes from the voices around us. We do not carry the weight of God's disapproval. It's not that we don't measure up to God. Rather, we don't measure up to what the world or church or pastor or youth minister or parent or teacher or overly zealous friend with a selectively 'marked up' Bible *tells* us is what God requires. All the while, if we listen closely, we will hear God asking us, "Who told you that you are naked? Who told you that there is something wrong with the way I created you? Who told you there is something wrong with the way I intended you to be?"

Peter, one of Jesus' original twelve disciples, was as impetuous as a third grader who felt he had all the right answers. You know the type. The teacher asks a question and scans the room of stupefied students. All are sitting and praying they will not be chosen to answer the posed problem. All of them but one. It's the one kid that has his hand stretched toward the sky, his other hand propping it up as if his raised arm weighs a ton and the wait is excruciatingly painful. He is verbally begging to be called upon by repeatedly grunting, "Ooo, Ooo, Ooo, Ooo. I know! I know! I know!" That's Peter.

In the middle of a storm, in the middle of the night, in the middle of the Sea of Galilee, Jesus walks on the water toward the disciples' boat. While others are cowered in quiet fear, Peter has his arm raised toward the dark, cloudy sky screaming, "Ooo, Ooo, Ooo. I want to try that!" Seated on the stones that line the hillside of Cesearea Phillipi, Jesus asks his disciples, "Who do you say that I am?" Knowledgeable about the world's view of Jesus, the disciples are less secure in their own answers. Silence dominates the moment until Peter raises his hand and says, "Ooo, Ooo, Ooo. I know, I know. I know. You are the Christ, the son of the living God!"

This impetuousness was a part of who Peter was created to be. Jesus did not demand this part of his character be renounced or altered. In fact, in Acts 2, on the day of Pentecost, all of the disciples are touched by the Holy Spirit. It is Peter, however, who throws up his hand. "Ooo, Ooo, Ooo. I have something to say!" And the impetuous disciple delivers the church's first sermon.

One of the first adjectives attached to Saul (later known as the Apostle Paul) is 'zealous.' As a Hebrew of Hebrews and a Pharisee of Pharisees, he zealously persecuted the early Christian believers. Upon his conversion, this overabundance of zealousness was not diminished or discarded. No other Christian in New Testament literature was more zealous than Paul in the defense and delivery of the gospel.

All of those who were called by Christ continued to be exactly who they were. By retaining their unique quirks and bends, they continued to reflect God's intention in their life. This freedom to 'live and be' that the disciples experienced also belongs to each one us as God's precious and peculiar creations.

Who told you that you were naked? Who told you there is something wrong with the way God created you? As human beings, we reflect the image of God, we reflect the limits of God, and reflect God's good intentions for all of us. No mixed messages.

Salvation

My family sat on the second pew. Maggie Pearson sat directly behind us on the third pew. We transported her to church each Sunday in our blue VW van. She was old. But, everyone seemed old to me back then. Since twenty of these people are still worshipping here today — 30 plus years later — they couldn't have been as old as I thought they were back then. But Maggie Pearson was old. She walked with a cane or walker, smelled like mentholatum ointment and, best of all, had a seemingly endless supply of Juicy Fruit gum in her purse.

Sunday school had ended early on one particular Sunday. I made my way down the short hallway, stopped in at the men's restroom, then hung a left into the sanctuary and settled into my pew with a few extra minutes to spare. The pinewood beneath my bottom had barely gotten warm when I felt a tap on my shoulder. I turned to give Ms. Pearson my attention and she asked, "Jimmy are you saved?"

Honestly? I didn't know. I had spent more than one afternoon sitting on a John Deere lawn mower, cutting circles in our front yard, praying and hoping that God would save me and make it certain enough that I would feel saved. But I felt nothing. I sat in the closet of my bedroom and prayed. I laid in bed at night and prayed. Nothing. I focused on repentance. I tried to recall and recant of all my sins, but at the ripe old age of 12 (and living in a small town) I just hadn't had that much opportunity to be bad! And most of my sins had already been atoned for at the end of a peach tree switch. I just figured I didn't need to be healed of those sins by Jesus' stripes since I had already gotten a few stripes of my own!

I read the Roman Road — Romans 3:23, 6:23 and Romans 10:9-10,13 — over and over again. I read the evangelical tracts that were stacked on a table in the narthex of the church. I prayed the sinner's prayer and the Lord's prayer and a whole bunch of my own prayers. Nothing.

I answered Ms. Pearson, "I don't know."

She responded, "Well, you can know right now."

She started with John 3:16, made her way down the familiar verses of the Roman Road, and ended up at Revelation 3:20 with Jesus standing at the door of my heart and knocking. She asked me if I wanted to be a Christian and I nodded affirmatively. She told me to bow my head and repeat a prayer after her. Line by line she spoke the sinners prayer and I repeated every word,

"Dear Lord Jesus, I know that I am a sinner, and I ask for Your forgiveness. I believe You died for my sins and rose from the dead. I turn from my sins and invite You to come into my heart and life. I want to trust and follow You as my Lord and Savior. In Your Name. Amen."

She looked up at me and asked, "Jimmy, are you saved?"

"I don't *feel* any different," I responded.

"You don't have to *feel* anything.' she said, "You just have to mean what you've prayed. God will welcome you into his heaven if you meant that prayer… and I'll give you a whole pack of Juicy Fruit."

"I'm saved!"

(My soul for a pack of chewing gum…)

The Philippian jailor asked the question, "What must I do to be saved?" The rich young ruler queried

Jesus about how he might inherit eternal life. I was a twelve-year-old boy — wandering and wondering. How do we answer this question today?

Most of us fall back upon the language we received as children even if that language feels limited, inadequate, and maybe even inaccurate. If you grew up evangelical like me, formulaic routes to eternal salvation are nothing new to you. We've heard the ABCs of Salvation: A — admit you are a sinner, B — believe in your heart the truth about Jesus, and C — confess your belief publically. We've also trotted down the aforementioned Roman Road: Romans 3:23 — "All have sinned and fallen short of the glory of God," Romans 6:23 — "The wages of sin is death...," Romans 10:9-10 — "If we confess with our mouths the Lord Jesus Christ and believe in our hearts God has raised him from the dead, we shall be saved," and Romans 10:13 — "Whoever calls upon the name of the Lord shall be saved." In addition to these familiar treks, there are numerous tracts, booklets, and canned, memorized conversations that convey the same material: admit you are a sinner, believe in Jesus, publically profess your belief through baptism...and presto chango...you're saved. (And in my case, I got a pack of chewing gum!)

It may be easier for some, but I found the first step of this process to be difficult. It was hard to 'admit I was a sinner.' Don't get me wrong, I'm not perfect today nor did I consider myself perfect then. And I digested as much of the concept of 'original sin' as a twelve-year-old boy has the capacity to chew on. But for some reason, this label felt inconsistent with the treatment I had received from my faith community, as well as, the image I assumed God saw when he looked at me. Sunday school lesson after Sunday school lesson had reinforced how 'special' I was to God. Children's sermon after children's sermon had informed me how much God loved me. Chorus after chorus rang out how precious I was in God's sight. But then, all of a sudden, I was supposed to recast myself as a sinner, dangling by a thread, held loosely between the index finger and thumb of a wrathful God over the fiery flames of an eternal hell. It was confusing.

Now, I knew a few people who could carry this label well. There was a bully on our street who tormented me daily. Three doors down was a teenage girl — just a few years older than I — who I had heard was loose. (I wasn't sure what that meant at the time, but I assumed it qualified her for 'admitting she was a sinner.') And I knew a few kids at school that had started smoking cigarettes — both the legal kind and the illegal kind. All of these folk might have qualified for a 'sinner label.' But even then, I had problems envisioning them to be anything but heaven-loved, wayward children who deserved a good lecture or a timeout. I just couldn't fathom the God who 'so loved the world' dangling any one of them over an eternity of torment. And I certainly couldn't imagine him dangling me there!

As the years passed, this 'starting point' on the path of salvation made less and less sense to me. The more I read the whole of scripture it made less and less sense to me. And the more I got to know my God — through study and prayer and conversations with my faith community — it made less and less sense to me. Why was I so uncomfortable with depravity as the starting point of salvation?

Julie Andrew's legendary performance as Maria, in *The Sound of Music*, included the performance of a trite little song titled "Do-Re-Mi." I have found the opening lines of that song to be quite informative with regard to the process and experience of salvation. Julie Andrews sang, "Let's start at the very beginning; a very good place to start." This was the problem in

Christian theology as it had been shared with me. My early mentors were beginning in Romans 3 and in Genesis 3. Romans 3 was the beginning of the Roman Road — "All have sinned..." Genesis 3 was the story of Adam and Eve's consumption of the forbidden fruit — traditionally interpreted as the Fall of Humankind. Both chapters were quoted to highlight our sinfulness and prepare us for the obvious necessary act of repentance or change. They were the designated starting points of understanding the means of establishing a relationship with God. But why not start at the beginning? Why not start in Genesis 1 or Romans 1? Wouldn't that be a "very good place to start?" Wouldn't that be the sensible place to start?

I now consider myself a Genesis 1 and Romans 1 kind of Christian. I've come to understand my own relationship with God in terms I believe to be truer and healthier. I've also been able to share the good news of God's love; and it truly sounds like good news! So when I'm asked, 'How does a person become a Christian?' my answer begins this way...

Remember who and whose you are.

As we've already affirmed in the chapter on humanity, every human being on the face of the earth is already a child of God. We have been created in God's image. We have God's holy DNA surging through our essence. We are a part of God's spiritual genetic code. We are the spitting image of the Holy God of the universe!

Not only are we God's children, but God is pretty darn proud of us! As pastor James Moore says in the title of one of his sermon compilation books, "If God has a refrigerator, your picture is on it!" When we were created, we were not perfect. We were never intended to be self-sustaining without flaw. But God looked upon us and proclaimed us 'good.' God loves us.

This immense love for and claim upon us is vocalized in our favorite verses of Bible and song. "For God so loved the world…" is one of the earliest memorized verses for many children within the circle of Christian faith. And before we learn that Bible verse, we've already learned the song, "Jesus loves me, this I know…." The memory we must plumb, however, is deeper and older than even our childhoods. It's a primeval truth embedded in the echoes of creation that resound in every created human being — we are created in God's image. We are good. We belong to God. The echoes can still be heard ringing in the air at our baptisms. "This is my beloved child, in whom I am well pleased." Those words were not spoken over Jesus *because* he was being baptized. They were spoken because they were already true. Jesus' baptism simply affirmed what was already true. The same is true for our baptisms. Salvation and eternal life begin when we remember who and whose we are. The truth of our identity and our heavenly parentage, however, is true whether we acknowledge it or not!

In Romans 1, the Apostle Paul writes, "…since the creation of the world his [God's] eternal power and divine nature, invisible though they are, have been understood and seen through the things he has made." Paul reminds us that the God who loves us has not been slack in calling to us. In a multitude of places and in a multitude of ways, God is like any loving parent, making efforts to draw us to God's self. God wants to enjoy us. And God desperately wants us to enjoy life with him. God wants us to know who and whose we are.

I was attending graduate school in Atlanta, Georgia when my birth mother located me. It was a Sunday afternoon. The telephone rang and I answered it as I had answered it on a hundred other rings and occasions. The voice on the other end of the line asked, "Is this Jimmy Dant?" I immediately knew it was someone from my childhood. I responded, "This is Jim Dant." She announced, "I'm your mother." In the course of the conversation, she asked what I was doing with my life. I told her I was an Associate Minister in a local church and completing a doctorate at a nearby seminary. When she asked what I was studying, I told her of my longtime love for Hebrew language and Hebrew scriptures. She began to cry. "You don't know who you are, do you?" she asked. After a long pause, she continued, "You were raised Roman Catholic because my second husband was Roman Catholic. You were four when I married him and I agreed to raise you according to his faith tradition. But Jimmy, you are Jewish. I am Jewish. Your grandparents are Jewish. Your great grandparents are Jewish." In a moment, I remembered who and whose I am. In many ways it changed my life.

What if you received a phone call like that today? What if the voice on the other line told you he was your real father? What if he finally identified himself as....Warren Buffet? (I'm in no way accusing Mr. Buffet of having illegitimate children wandering around the world. I'm just using his name in order to take illustrative advantage of the immensity of his wealth.) If you found out you were Mr. Buffet's child, wouldn't it significantly change your life? The wisdom and resources at your disposal would be enormous!

You are one of God's children. Always have been. Always will be. You have God's DNA flowing through your very being. You've been created in God's image. You carry God's features. You look kind of like God. You are inherently good. You have access to God's great wisdom and God's great storehouse of care. Remember who and whose you are. This one acknowledgment connects you to the God who has never stopped loving and caring for you. This is the beginning of salvation.

Relax into the unconditional love and grace of God.

A couple of verses from Ephesians is the most common detour from the Roman Road when navigating the old path of salvation. Inevitably, the new convert will need to be informed...

> For by grace you have been saved through faith, and this is not your own doing; it is the gift of God — not the result of works, so that no one may boast. (Ephesians 2:8-9)

Ironically, as a child it felt like I was doing a lot of 'doing' to be saved. It did feel like a lot of work! I had to listen to 'the plan of salvation.' I had to admit that I was a sinner. I had to repent of my sins. I had to believe. I had to pray a sinner's prayer. I had to confess my faith by walking down the aisle of the church. I had to be baptized. Now, to be fair, at many points along the way I was informed that this particular 'work' is not necessary for your salvation. (And I quote...) "You don't 'have' to walk down the aisle to be saved, but the Bible does say 'whoever confesses me before men, him will I confess before my father which is in heaven.' Why wouldn't you want to walk the aisle and confess God before your church family?" The road to salvation, while built upon grace, was paved with doing: admitting, believing, repenting, praying, confessing, walking, and being baptized.

Instead of all this work, what would it be like to simply relax into the unconditional love of God? Let's truly make this a gift from God. Let's honestly allow God to save us without us doing a thing. Let's not work *for* this or work *at* this.

If there is a 'moment' of salvation, it is when I remember that I am already a child of God. It is that moment that I remember who and whose I am. Everything else will happen naturally as I begin to live with and love the God of my salvation. I will want to get to know the God I've ignored for so long and I'll want God to know me. I will pray. I will choose to do good and right actions that come from a motivation of genuine love. I will change. In my prayers, I will certainly share the struggles of my life. I will listen for God's voice. I will read the testimonies and stories of my family members found in biblical literature and I'll become familiar with their interactions with God. I will want others to know that I have found my parent God. I will want to go to family reunions every Sunday morning and enjoy the brothers and sisters I never knew were related to me. None of this occurs in an effort to please or appease God. It's just what we do when we are family.

All of these 'works' very genuinely occurred after my biological mother found me. We talked. I met other family members. I asked them what they knew and how they had experienced my mother. I told other people about my mother. I relaxed into the relationship.

The gospel is supposed to be good news. Well, here's some good news for you. We can't get this wrong. Really! We cannot eternally mess up with God. We are God's children and God unconditionally loves us! I have three daughters. There are at least three things about my relationship with them that are permanently settled. The first is, there is nothing they could ever do that would cause me to stop loving them. Nothing. I've heard other parents say, 'If my child ever _____ (you fill in the blank), I would disown him or her!' I cannot say that about my children. No matter where they go, what they do, who they love, or what they say, I will always love them. Even if they reject my love or deny me their love, I will still love them. They are the only things in this world that I've had a part in creating. I love them unconditionally. Now, wouldn't it be arrogant of me to think that I could love my children to a greater degree than God loves God's children. The Apostle Paul wrote these words to the church at Ephesus...

> I pray that you may have the power to comprehend, with all the saints, what is the breadth and length and height and depth, and to know the love of Christ that surpasses knowledge... (Ephesians 3:18-19a)

I can imagine and know a love that never ends. I have that kind of love for my children. God loves us with an even greater love beyond our imagination!

The second thing that is settled with regard to my children is that I want them to be themselves. I do not want them shaping their lives in order to please me. I do not want them accommodating my interests, appeasing my needs, and engaging my pursuits at the cost of their own passions. I want them to find themselves and then let me enjoy them for who they are. While each of them has respectively displayed a hint of interest in Hebrew, running, and music (my primary passions), they only 'resemble' me in these areas. For the most part, their passions are elsewhere because they've forged their own lives. They are jumping out of airplanes, laughing at sitcoms, and cheering at major league baseball games. None of these activities are a part of my pattern of living, but I love who my children have become. I enjoy seeing them enjoy the life I've given them.

Finally, I do not expect my children to be perfect. And of course, they have not disappointed me in this area! Our imperfection is a given. In fact, it's a misnomer to think that we were created perfect in the Garden of Eden. At no point in biblical literature is this affirmed. We were created 'good.' And we were created 'innocent.' But we were not and are not and cannot be perfect. We were created to be human. That's what we are at our best. Whatever we imagine the perfect relationships with God, others and self to be, we aren't going to be able to attain it. We are human. To do anything less than simply be human is to start thinking we can be like God again and that puts us back at square one.

When the Bible admonishes us to 'be perfect even as God is perfect,' it is not adjuring us to be like God. Rather, we are being encouraged to be who we are. God is perfectly God. God lives the role of God because that is who God is. God accepts and adheres to God's role in the cosmos. We are called to live the role of God's children — humans. That's how we perfectly live out our lives. We are perfectly living our lives when we live as imperfect human beings dependent upon the grace of God! We cannot get this wrong. Relax into the unconditional love of God. It is in the relaxing that admissions, beliefs, prayers, and confessions are formed. It is when we relax that living takes the place of striving, relationship takes the place of groveling, and love takes the place of fearful doubt.

Relax into the unconditional love of God. When we are truly relaxed into the caring arms of God, it is easy for us to trust that God will carry us wherever we need to go in this journey. We will be saved and safe.

Share this good news with others.

My personal pilgrimage has taken me from an unpracticed Judaism to a practiced Roman Catholicism to a Baptist profession of faith. Having been primarily shaped in the Baptist tradition, I'm an evangelical. I can't shake it. I haven't tried real hard. But can't shake it nonetheless. I sense a need — a heavenly commission — to share the faith I enjoy with others. This sense of commission, however, is not the most compelling factor in my evangelical urge. I'm primarily motivated by how truly good and graceful and freeing this gospel really is. I wish someone had shared these words with me as a teenager or younger adult. Maybe I could have avoided a load of shame and guilt and struggle. Maybe I could have better enjoyed the abundant wisdom and resources of God. Maybe I could have just lived with a deeper sense of being gracefully loved.

I shared this revised 'plan of salvation' at a conference for young ministers several years ago. Eyes either welled with tears or lit with excitement. Finally one young minister spoke, "I've tried to share this type message with people in my life, but many of them will not listen. They are not willing to change. Even some of my Christian friends are unwilling to accept a God that is this loving and graceful. What can we say to them? How do we convince them this message is true?" I heard his frustration. I've felt the same frustration with regard to friends and family members and fellow faith journeyers. I believe the answer is in the timing.

Most people are very *settled* in their faith or their lack thereof. The structures of their life and the routines of their day are comfortable. This can be true for the person established in vocation, as well as, a person established in an addiction. Each believes that life is moving along as it should be. Introducing the idea of 'conversion' at this point in their journey is rarely fruitful. There is no perceived need for change and few arguments that would convince otherwise.

Our openness to change or conversion typically occurs during those seasons when life feels *unsettled.* The pain of a tragedy, the uncertainty of entering adolescence, the adjustments to the birth of a child, the failures inherent in relationships and occupations, and the inevitable moments of loss. These and other crises cultivate a space in our lives for new possibilities to be entertained. It is at this point that the good news of the gospel has the best opportunity to be heard and embraced. This should in no way be understood as manipulating people in the tender times of their lives. It is simply the way we are built. It's the way we operate. If the graceful, unconditional love of God is not integrated into our lives during these times, some other presumably stabilizing factor or relationship will be. It has been my experience that God's graceful presence is the only reliable place to *resettle.* This is where we recognize who and whose we are. Even then, we will resettle in our understanding of God many times.

This process of being settled, becoming unsettled and resettling is an inevitable, healthy life pattern. As previously stated, it will often happen in the natural course of life. Life happens. Crises occur. At other times, we can intentionally move ourselves into unsettled space for the purposes of deepening our understanding of and dependence upon God. This often happens when persons go on retreat, enter seminary, engage the Ignatian exercises, journey into what St. John of the Cross called 'the dark night of the soul' — an intentional journey of relinquishing all that we think we know of God so that we might know God in a deeper way. All of these paths provide a season of unsettling so that we might resettle in closer intimacy with God. In Philippians 2:12, the Apostle Paul encouraged the Philippian Christians to 'work out their salvation.' Conversion then, is a series of crises — chosen and unchosen — that move us from being settled, to unsettled, to a place of resettling. Conversion is a process and a lifetime journey.

Salvation. It's simply a matter of remembering who and whose you are, relaxing into the unconditional love of God, and then sharing that growth process with the rest of the world.

I realize I haven't mentioned the 'threat of hell' once in this chapter. I further realize that the mention of hell has long played a pivotal role in prompting persons to embark upon the journey of salvation and faith. Allow me then, to end with this word — every day we spend not recognizing who and whose we are and every day we spend not relaxing into the unconditional love of God is a day we spend in hell. Enough said.

God

Driving east away from Northside Baptist Church in Eudora, I pass a large empty plot of land on my right just across the railroad track. I turn and allow my rental car to ease onto the backside of the empty tract.

I grew up in a sawmill family. I was adopted as a third grader. My biological parents were not able to adequately care for me. So my biological father's sister and her husband adopted me. My aunt became my mother, my father became my uncle, my uncle became my father, and my mother became my aunt. All the men worked at the sawmill.

My grandfather owned the hardwood mill where all the men worked. The mill primarily cut oak, hickory, and cherry. Pappa didn't like softwood pines. He said pine lumber 'gummed up the saw blades' and brought a much lower price in the lumber market. So he only processed hardwood. My grandfather not only owned the mill, but he worked there. He was the carriage operator. He sat in a small booth in a large building. Just below him was a carriage — a small train car that rolled back and forth on a small stretch of track (maybe 60 feet long). The carriage held a horizontal log that rolled back and forth against a vertical band saw. From the booth, my Pappa could control the direction of the carriage as well as mechanically control a contraption of the carriage that turned the log allowing boards to be cut from all sides. The carriage was run by steam. It made wonderful hissing and sputtering noises as it rolled back and forth along the track.

My biological father was the lumber inspector. He walked a conveyer belt where every piece of lumber my Pappa cut would pass his scrutinizing eye. A long stick with a piece of blue chalk on the end allowed my dad to grade and mark each board. He had to flip most pieces of lumber to best inspect the quality. He never bent over and flipped them with his hand. Instead he had perfected a system of flipping the board with the end of his steel-toed work boot. He had a hole in the toe of his work boot where the leather was worn all the way down to the steel.

My adoptive father was the saw filer. When the large band saws eventually got dull or hit a nail that had been hammered into a tree, the saw would have to be sharpened. My adoptive father would take the band saw that was about 15 feet in circumference, place it on a horizontal rack, and file each tooth to its expected degree of sharpness. Add to these three men all the mechanics, assistants, office personnel, and yardmen (the men who stacked the finished lumber) and you have the people who used to work on this now empty tract of land about a mile east of Northside Baptist Church.

In the summers, my grandfather would hire his two oldest grandsons (that would include me) to stack lumber in the lumber yard. We were yardmen. Temperatures would climb to over one hundred degrees in our little delta town. The crisscrossed stacks of lumber would climb to nearly eight feet. On our lunch breaks, my grandfather would come to visit us as we lay resting atop a stack of lumber, eating bologna sandwiches accompanied by some Cheetos, sipping Dr. Peppers and trying our best to cool off from several hours of tossing boards. My Pappa would smile at our industrious exhaustion and say to us, "One day this will all be yours." Little did my Pappa know how large and powerful the competing industrial mills would become. I was in college when I heard the family mill was closed and demolished.

Today I'm standing on an empty tract of land. I'm sad the mill is gone but glad that it's not all mine. Little did my Pappa know how much I hated working at the sawmill. But today, I miss it.

My grandmother used to laugh at all her boys — her husband, son, son-in-law, and grandsons. She said we had sawdust in our veins and would never be able to separate ourselves from the smell and feel of lumber. Maybe she was right. To this day, when I'm driving through the small southern towns of Georgia, Alabama, Mississippi, or Arkansas with the car window rolled down, I can smell the air and tell if there is a sawmill operating there. I can even distinguish between the smell of a softwood mill and a hardwood mill.

I visited a winery in Napa Valley, California last year. As part of the tour, we were ushered into the barrel room where hundreds of barrels of wine were stacked, stored, and aging to perfection. I could smell the wood of the barrels. Our guide told us the barrels were made in France, from a particular type of wood and cost hundreds of dollars. I wandered from the group and ran my hand along the smooth wood of the barrels. I touch wood and smell wood everywhere I go.

When someone starts explaining God to me, I usually run. I am not a systematic theologian. In fact, both words push against my grain. I'm not very systematic about anything in life — I float. I'm also not much of a theologian. I find it hard to talk about God and to find language that I can comfortably apply to God. I'm typically more frustrated with what people say about God in theology than I am my own experience of God. And that's why I run. I am not a theologian, but I touch God and smell God everywhere I go.

So what am I comfortable saying about God? What can be said that won't make you bolt from the pages of this book?

God is mysterious.

If this were all a person said to me about God, I would not run. God is mysterious. I am comfortable with a God that cannot be nailed down with firm language and consistent attributes. I'm comfortable understanding all language about God as metaphors that describe an experienced characteristic of God, but at the same time, are not literally accurate. God is a king but also a servant. God is a rock but also a breath. God is a covenant keeper but also divorces (Jeremiah 3). God is truth but also a liar (1 Kings 22). God is life and also a killer (Leviticus 10, 2 Samuel 6, Acts 5). God cannot be completely bound by our descriptive terms. God is mysterious.

I'm comfortable with a God who operates on a whim, is predictably unpredictable and bears more human qualities than most folk of faith would like to admit. Theological terms that make me want to run, like omnipotent, omnipresent, and omniscient are hardly descriptive of the God we find in scripture. They impose upon God certain superlative features that God rarely exhibits. They probably describe the kind of God we think we want, but not necessarily the God we've actually got!

While one could argue the finer points of what it means to be omniscient, God doesn't always act as if he knows everything. In Genesis 6, God 'regrets' the creation of humankind and decides to cleanse the earth of them with a flood. After the flood, he 'regrets' causing a flood. Is it possible to 'regret' if one is omniscient? In Genesis 19, God has to 'go down and see what is happening' in Sodom and Gomorrah. It would seem that omniscience and omnipresence would have taken care of that little chore. In Exodus

32 and in the story of Jonah, God 'changes God's mind' about actions God fully intended to perform. Can an omniscient mind change? Is it really a change if you knew you were going to change? If you knew you were going to change, then it's not really a change since you already knew what you would eventually do. Okay, now I'm being facetious, but I think you get the point. Our theological descriptions conveniently deliver us from having to face the unmanageable truths about God. They diminish the mystery. And I like the mystery.

I'm comfortable with a God who chooses to be hidden even amid the greatest moments of self-revelation. God came to Moses and the children of Israel as fire and cloud. God came to Abraham and Jacob in the person of strangers and to Belshazzar (Daniel 5) as strange fingers writing on the king's wall. God comes as wind and a dove and a still small voice. The one time God decides to reveal self more fully to Moses, Moses only gets his backside and not a frontal view. There is a hiddenness even in God's revelation. God is mysterious. And I like the mystery.

I can actually imagine the church focusing on mystery rather than the management of God. Worship would be an adoration of mystery.

Education would be an exploration of mystery — no holds barred. Evangelism would be a sharing of mystery where we admit we don't have all the answers, but would love to struggle alongside the world with all the questions. This would be a huge change for us. In many churches, worship is the management of God's glory. Pastors and priests use carefully crafted litanies and lines to accurately convey approved affirmations about God. We shape God by the Psalms we choose to read, the hymns we choose to sing, and the language adopted in sermons. When was the last time we read an 'angry Psalm' in morning worship? Have the words of Psalm 137 ever rung through our church's rafters? Is there a time when it needs to be read?

> Remember, O Lord, against the Edomites
> the day of Jerusalem's fall, how they said,
> "Tear it down! Tear it down! Down to
> its foundations!" O daughter Babylon,
> you devastator! Happy shall they be who
> pay you back what you have done to us!
> Happy shall they be who take your little
> ones and dash them against the rock!
> (Psalm 137:7-9)

When was the last time we lamented in corporate worship? Does the congregation ever have a right to vent its deepest complaints to God with no quick reverential apologies to follow? If we haven't engaged this ancient form of prayer, we've ignored the book of Lamentations and about a third of the Psalms!

We manage God in worship. We manage God in the church's educational systems and evangelical endeavors. We teach our children and the world an appropriate theological understanding of God. Couched in creed and doctrine are the safe words we want people to know and hold and believe. And while all these words are good — don't hear me wrong, I love and cling to the sacred words of the church — it must be stated that God is not always safe. God is mysterious and uncontrollable. We were never intended to contain God in our phrases and in our hearts. We were intended to surrender ourselves and fall faithfully into the arms of a God we cannot fully understand.

God is mysterious and I'm comfortable falling into that mystery.

God is gracefully persistent.

I am comfortable with God's mystery and I'm grateful for God's graceful persistence. In the biblical story, God never gives up on the redemption of humankind even though it's a threat that gets tossed around every once in a while. In Genesis 3, Adam and Eve eat of the forbidden fruit. God had threatened death, but he gracefully grants life. God was persistent in the hope that the created ones would love their creator.

As the biblical record continues, God floods the earth, but in graceful persistence delivers one family in hopes they might repopulate this world with a people in love with their God. In fact, God is so gracefully persistent, in 1 Peter 3:18-20, the crucified Christ enters into Hell and delivers the disobedient who were killed in the ancient flood of Noah.

> For Christ also suffered for sins once for all, the righteous for the unrighteous, in order to bring you to God. He was put to death in the flesh, but made alive in the spirit, in which also he went and made a proclamation to the spirits in prison, who

in former times did not obey, when God
waited patiently in the days of Noah,
during the building of the ark, in which
a few, that is, eight persons, were saved
through water. (1 Peter 3:18-20)

God is gracefully persistent. God continues
throughout the biblical story to convince humanity
of his love for them and garner the love of humanity
for himself. God gives the law to Moses in hopes the
law would establish a loving and lasting relationship.
When the law was not followed, God sent prophets
in hopes they might redirect people toward the God
who loved them. When all else failed, God sent his
only son into the world. If God is anything, God is
gracefully persistent.

My childhood pastor loved to tell the story of the
little bird that lost his way during migration. It seems
a little bird appeared on the window ledge of a lady's
home. The bitter winds of winter had already begun
to blow and the lady knew the bird had lost its way
while heading south. She cleverly thought, "I'll write
the bird a note." So she allowed her breath to fog the
window pane where the little bird was sitting. With
her index finger she printed in the moisture of her

breath — Fly South. The little bird did not budge. Other birds were passing over her home in the complex patterns and synchronizations with which flocks fly. She screamed at the little bird, "Listen to the other birds above you. Follow them." But the little bird still did not budge. Finally, in frustration, the woman thought to herself, "If only I could become a bird, I could tell him."

God is gracefully persistent and I do not believe God will give up on us until the whole of creation is redeemed. This certainly seems to be Jesus' understanding of God. In Luke 15, Jesus tells a series of three parables: the parable of the lost sheep, the parable of the lost coin, and the parable of the prodigal son. In each of these parables, something is lost and must be found. And in each of these parables, the search does not end until the lost item is found. The shepherd never gives up in his search for the one, final, lost sheep. The woman, while holding nine coins, does not stop searching until she finds the tenth. The prodigal father searches the horizon for his son until his prodigal son comes home. And after that, the father is still not satisfied until his elder son is celebrating at the table as well. God never gives up on us. God is gracefully persistent.

God is not that impressive.

I hope this assertion doesn't overly disturb you. It is, however, true. God is not that impressive. Perhaps this is the reason God chooses to be so persistent!

God is not impressive. God does not impress God's self upon us. Yes, we are created in the image of God. But God never demands that we acknowledge and adhere to that image. God does not fix an idea in our minds or apply external pressure to our lives in order to conform us to his will. The biblical story does not present to us a coercive God. Rather, we seem to have all the free will we want — maybe a little more than we want. In this way, God is not impressive.

But God is also not impressive in the more common use of the term. There is nothing about God that is overly attractive. There is no attribute of God or action performed by God that has an inordinate amount of pull on our lives. Moses turned aside to meet God in a burning bush. From that bush, God called Moses to deliver the people of Israel from slavery in Egypt. Even in that moment, however, Moses needed a name, and proof and a promise of God's presence and assistance. Later, when Moses requested release of the captives, Pharaoh was not impressed with God's signs or miracles or words.

In 1 Kings 19, the prophet Elijah is searching for God's presence in a cave on Mt. Horeb. Elijah steps outside the cave to see the brute force of an impressive wind that is so strong it crumbled a portion of the mountain. The text maintains, however, God was not in the wind. Following the wind, Elijah felt the rumble of an earthquake. God was not in the earthquake. And after the earthquake, a blazing fire streaked across the side of the mountain. God was not in the heat of the fire. After nature had performed all her impressive displays, God was found in the silence. God simply isn't that impressive.

This unimpressive streak continues in the second person of the Trinity, God's son, Jesus Christ. We don't usually speak of Jesus in these terms, but it's true. God in Christ was not really that impressive. For centuries, Christians have claimed Isaiah 53 as a prophecy concerning the appearance of the Messiah. Have you read it carefully...or even casually?

> ...he had no form or majesty that we should look at him, nothing in his appearance that we should desire him.

He was despised and rejected by others;
a man of suffering and acquainted with
infirmity; and as one from whom others
hide their faces he was despised, and we
held him of no account. (Isaiah 53:2b-3)

The prophecy we embrace concerning Jesus essentially says he was nothing to look at. He was nothing to be desired. He was one from whom people would turn their faces. Jesus was not impressive.

Jesus did not enter this world in an impressive fashion. He was not born to royalty or in elaborate surroundings. He did not live an impressive life. Jesus' father was a carpenter and his mother a young girl who had gotten pregnant before marriage. Jesus grew up in the little town of Nazareth. He spent the majority of his vocational life in the rural region of Galilee. During his short ministry, multitudes occasionally gathered around him. And yet, Jesus neither said nor did anything that maintained the crowd's attention. They always eventually dispersed. In fact, at the end of John 6, so many disciples had deserted Jesus that he turned to the twelve and asked if they too were going to leave him. Jesus wasn't that impressive.

Not even the resurrection of Jesus was earth shat-
tering. Think about it. This is the resurrection of the
only begotten Son of God. Nothing like this had ever
happened on the face of the earth. One might expect
the earth to shake, some fireworks to be shot off, and
maybe a homecoming parade planned. After all, if
people saw the fanfare, maybe it would have been
easier for them to believe. But, this is not God's way.
Jesus was resurrected in the quiet, stillness of a Sunday
morning. No one was there. No one saw. When the
angel and a few people did decide to visit the tomb,
all they found were neatly folded grave clothes.
Unimpressive. This shouldn't surprise us, however.
In Luke 15, Jesus tells the famous story of the rich
man and Lazarus. The rich man dies and goes to hell.
Lazarus dies soon after and is carried to the restful
bosom of Father Abraham. The rich man lifts up his
eyes from hell and implores Abraham to send Lazarus
back to earth in order to convince his remaining
siblings to mend their ways. Abraham responds by
assuring the rich man his remaining siblings have the
law and the prophets — the scriptures — and that
should be plenty for generating faith. The rich man
then presents a seemingly compelling argument. The
scriptures aren't impressive enough. But if someone

were to rise from the dead, that would convince his brothers of the error of their ways. Resurrection would be impressive. Abraham finally responds by telling the rich man that if they will not believe the scriptures, they will not believe if someone rises from the dead. Resurrection just isn't that impressive. God, in Christ, just isn't that impressive.

Like the rich man, you may wish to argue. You may want to posit miracle after miracle and teaching after teaching to build a case for the impressive work of God. The truth, however, is very clear. Parting the water or walking on water, a fish swallowing Jonah or a crowd fed with two fish, the healing of a leper or the raising of the dead…nothing that God does on God's own or in the person of Jesus Christ was ever impressive enough to keep the crowds committed. No miracle is impressive enough to generate sustained faith. Everyone watches for a while, listens for a while, follows for a while, then shrugs his or her shoulders and walks away. God really isn't that impressive.

Perhaps this is why God is so gracefully persistent. God will not impose God's self upon us. And God will not try to impress us into a loving relationship by showing off a miracle or two. God leaves us free to love on the basis of love alone.

Once we respond to this unimpressive, gracefully persistent, mysterious God, then...

God chooses to work with us and through us.

This has not always been the case. In the earliest chapters of the human story, God worked *on* us. God created humans. God commanded humans. God put humans out of the garden. God instructed Noah to build an Ark. God scattered the people of Babel. For the first eleven chapters of human history or at least the first eleven chapters of Genesis, God operated on humankind. God independently managed earthly life from the heavens.

All this changed in Genesis 12. God approached a man named Abraham and engaged him in God's work. God promised to bless the world *through* Abraham. God was no longer operating *on* us, but choosing to operate *through* us. This changed everything. Working through humanity is a messy proposition. We have to be shaped and formed for the tasks at hand. (God probably hadn't anticipated the difficulty of this process!) And when using

humans to accomplish heavenly tasks, God necessarily acquiesced to human limits and means. This
means God saved the world from famine through the
industrious strategies of Joseph. God delivered Israel
from Egypt through the leadership ability of Moses.
God protected Israel through the military might of
Joshua, Samson and David. Of course, therein lies
the problem. Once God adopts humanity's limits and
means, once God decides to work with and through
humans...God's hands get messy. Readers often
struggle with God's involvement in the messiness
of Old Testament wars. Some discount the recorded
involvement as Israel's retrospective interpretation of
God's presence because they believe a God of love
would not be involved in such activity. But, if God is
involved at all, it's because God chose to work with
and through humankind. At its worst, it comes to
war. At its best, this union of mission is exemplified
in humanity working for peace and justice in God's
world.

God chooses to work with and through us. This
can be a messy venture. It can certainly put God's rep-
utation at risk. But, it lifts our role in God's creation
to a whole new level. We are co-laborers with God.
We are the hands and feet of his Son Jesus Christ.

We are ambassadors of reconciliation in a torn and hurting world. Messy for God, maybe…but what an honor for us.

Daniel Lord, a Jesuit brother, voiced it this way in a prayer…

> For some strange reason, Lord, you
>   depend on me.
> What possible need could you have for
>   my shoulder?
> Why should you lean on me? Yet you do
>   just that.
>
> I am grateful. It is a challenge and a trust,
> an inspiration and a call to character.
>
> If you are willing to depend on me,
> weak and clumsy as I am,
> I am eager not to fail you.
>
> Lean on me, dear Lord.
> At least pretend to find me a help.
> May your sweet pretense
> make me worthy of your very real trust.

This unimpressive, mysterious, gracefully persistent God has chosen to work with and through us. What a God! And I touch God and smell God wherever I go.

Jesus

A portrait of Jesus hangs in the hallway just behind the baptistery of Northside Baptist Church. It's the *Head of Christ* portrait painted in 1941 by Warner Sallman. This famous portrait has been reproduced more than 500 million times and one of them found its way onto the wall of our church hallway. Gentle Jesus...gazing upward to the left. Poor Jesus. I'm certain my childhood memories are skewed, but my best recollection is: we birthed him at Christmas, disappointed him every day of our lives, and then beat the hell out of him just before Easter...and during every revival.

Once a year, I heard a lot about the birth of Jesus. The death of Jesus was urgently proclaimed all year long. I don't, however, remember that much about the life of Jesus. The stories were told in both sermon and song — healing, walking on water, and rebuking the Pharisees. But somehow these stories always seemed to be primers for beating him one more time, crucifying him, and then guilting me into following him more closely. For no matter what Jesus did in the course of his life, the fact that I couldn't emulate it put him right back on the cross. We were always in the process of birthing and dying...dying and being born again. The significance of Jesus' life somehow got lost in the valley between these two mountains.

This is not a criticism of my faith family, however. It is in fact, the most common conversation of the church. One need only look at the creeds of Christendom to note how centered we are on the birth and death of Jesus with little regard for all that happened in between. The Nicene Creed — approved by the council of Constantinople in A.D. 381 — states:

> ...he became incarnate from the Virgin Mary, and was made man. For our sake he was crucified under Pontius Pilate; he suffered death and was buried. On the third day he rose again...

The Augsburg Confession of Faith, submitted at the Diet of Augsburg in 1530 declares:

...was born of the Virgin Mary, truly suf-
fered, was crucified, dead, and buried...

Pick a creed, any creed, and most will make the
birth and death of Jesus dominant at the expense of
all the love and life he gave in between.

It's not only evident in our creeds, but it's also
vividly distinguished in the pattern of our worship.
For those churches that follow a liturgical worship
calendar, the seasons of Advent/Christmas and Lent/
Easter are holy days — holidays — with distinct
prayers and colors and traditions and songs. All
other days of the year are relegated to "Common"
time. And while we would theologically contend that
common time is just as special as the holy seasons...
we all know better. It's as if giving sight to a blind
man, cleansing the skin of a leper, defending and
sparing the life of an adulterer, welcoming a child,
praying in a garden, or giving a cup of cold water in
Jesus' name is a little less holy than the nativity or the
resurrection.

No one loves Christmas and Easter more than I
love them. I'm a holiday fanatic. But in recent years,
the more common days of his earthly existence have
become more and more meaningful to me. It is

within the whole scope of the gospel that I encounter truth about Jesus. His life is just as revealing as his birth, death, and resurrection. It is in his teaching and his living, not just the brackets of his life, that my ideas concerning his identity and my relevance to his life have been shaped.

I still cling to the idea that Jesus came to earth to help us understand what God is really like.

It's not a novel idea, but it's a solid one. Jesus told his disciples that when they looked at him they were looking at the Father. I get it. We get it. We see God in Jesus. Anglican theologian, Michael Ramsey, pushed this idea to the theological limit when he affirmed, "God is Christ-like and in him there is no un-Christ-likeness at all." Jesus came to help us understand what God is like.

As previously stated, God is multi-faceted. It is impossible to tie down the mysterious nature of God. This is practically reflected in the person of Jesus. There are those today who assume they can define Jesus in contemporary theological/political terms. Jesus is often described as being liberal or conservative, communal or capitalist, passive or militaristic.

Jesus, like God, cannot be confined to or defined by any of these labels. When any descriptive term begins to fit him comfortably, he shifts and pushes against the observer's vested interest.

When the Pharisees questioned Jesus' seemingly inappropriate activity on the Sabbath, Jesus responded with what they considered a liberal interpretation of the law — the Sabbath was made for humankind, not humankind for the Sabbath. Jesus had no aversion to healing or feeding on Sabbath. It cannot be concluded, however, that Jesus embraced a liberal agenda with regard to the law. For the moment the law was treated with even a hint of triviality, Jesus affirmed that not one jot or tittle or iota of the law would pass away, but must be fulfilled. Jesus is a reflection of the multi-faceted mystery of God.

Perhaps more important to our personal needs, Jesus is a reflection of God's desire to be with us. While there is much that is mysterious within the heart of God, it can be affirmed with much assurance that God desires relationship with us. Why else would the ancient God of Israel continually engage human creatures? Why else would God make deity vulnerable — be held in a mother's womb, born into the context of his creation, and become susceptible to the human experience? God desires to be with us. The angel's messages seem divergent, but in fact could not offer more clarity. To Joseph, the angel said, "You will name the child, Jesus." (Matthew 1:21) And later the angel said, "He will be called Emmanuel — God with us." (Matthew 1:23).

Jesus truly was "God with us." In being with us, God gave us the opportunity to understand more about God. Jesus sat at the feet of temple scholars when he was a twelve-year-old boy. Jesus learns with us and grows with us. God discovers. Jesus stood in a baptismal line with repentant sinners. Jesus hopes with us. God has dreams. Jesus turned wedding wash water into wonderful wine. Jesus rejoices with us. God provides. Jesus walked with fisherman, tax collectors, prostitutes, and religious leaders. Jesus journeys with us. God is interested in us. Jesus wept at the tomb of a friend. Jesus hurts with us. God sorrows. In the Garden of Gethsemane, Jesus sweat great drops of blood as he faced imminent death. Jesus struggles with us. God does not discount our fears. Jesus felt forsaken by God as he hung dying on a cross. Jesus questions with us. God does not judge our doubts, but enters into our quandaries. Pick any moment in Jesus' life and you will find God infusing heavenly presence into our temporal lives. God desires to be with us.

God truly is with us in Jesus and in Jesus we see what God is like. This, however, is not the only answer to the question. Why else would God make deity vulnerable — be held in a mother's womb, born into the context of his creation, and become susceptible to the human experience? Jesus wasn't just trying to show us what God is like...

Jesus was also God's attempt to understand what it's like to be human.

I've always thought it would be easy to be God. God sits in God's heaven and writes the laws — we are the ones who have to keep them. God sits in God's heaven and purposes a will — we are the ones who have to figure it out and follow. God sits in God's heaven and dreams a creation — we are the ones who have to tend it. God sits in God's heaven and destines life — we are the ones who have to live it. Admittedly, I'm oversimplifying the work of the Almighty, but I think you get the point. God is God. We are human. It's tough being us!

In the person of Jesus, God came to understand what it's like to be human. God did not engage the human experience as an observer; God had already been there. God became a participant. God became human. God subjected God's self to the human condition. In every aforementioned moment in Jesus' life, God allowed God's self to experience ignorance, hope, joy, frustration, sadness, loss, fear, doubt, and more.

As I've mentioned before, one of God's first observations with regard to humankind comes in Genesis 2:18, when God saw that the man was lonely. Since God lives in community as a triune God — Father, Son and Holy Spirit — is it possible that God saw the man's loneliness but had no sense of the loneliness? In the person of Jesus, God came to understand our loneliness and know our need for community. Could there be a lonelier human chapter than the hours before and during Jesus' crucifixion? Jesus was betrayed by Judas, denied by Peter, abandoned by the rest of his disciples and ultimately questioned God's presence in his dying moments. By the time Jesus drew his final breath, God knew the pain of human loneliness.

In Romans 8:34, the Apostle Paul tells the Romans that Jesus now sits at the right hand of the Father interceding for us. For me, it's a picture of Jesus constantly reminding the Father, "They are human...and we know what that's like."

Our understanding of God and God's understanding of us are wonderful motivations for God's entrance into this world in the person of Jesus. I do not, however, believe these to be the primary reasons for this incarnational moment. The offering of God's self in the life of Jesus meant something more.

Jesus was God's best expression of love toward us.

For years I tried to reconcile Jesus' life and death with God's love. My earliest understandings of Jesus' life — and particularly his death — did not fit well with the idea of a loving God. The pastors and teachers of my earliest Christian formation were strong advocates of substitutionary atonement. I never heard that specific label used, but the idea permeated almost every sermon preached and hymn we sang. I recognize that my description of this idea, as well as other atonement theories, will be grossly oversimplified. I'm simply trying to voice the concept through my youthful understanding. After all, that is the understanding that shaped the early tones of my theological voice. My best understanding of God's work in Christ was — I had sinned. My sin demanded that God's wrath be appeased. God's justice had to be satisfied through appropriate punishment. So, God, in his love, sent his son Jesus to die in my place. Jesus took the brunt of God's wrath and paid — in full — my debt to God. Jesus took my place. Substitutionary atonement.

It is musically expressed in the words of many familiar hymns:

> Up Calvary's mountain, one dreadful morn, walked Christ my Savior, weary and worn, facing for sinners death on the cross...

> Alas and did my Savior bleed and did my sovereign die. Would he devote that sacred head for sinners such as I?

> What can wash away my sin? Nothing but the blood of Jesus.

The message rang loud and clear in the words of my pastor, "The wages of sin is death. And Jesus died to pay the debt for your sins."

My oldest daughter struggled to understand the idea of atonement as well. Her wonderments and arguments were much simpler than mine, but just as valid. She mused aloud on more than one occasion, "If God is really God — I mean if God can do anything God wants — why can't he just forgive sin? Why does someone have to die in order for sin to be forgiven? If God is really God, can't he come up with a better system?" I've often thought the same thing. If God is the one who establishes the parameters of justice, then why would a loving God institute a system of forgiveness that demanded death?

Jesus died in my place. Substitutionary atonement.

Less frequently spoken — but still part of my childhood tradition — was the ransom atonement theory. Often referred to as the *Christus Victor* model, Jesus' death is considered a ransom paid to Satan in exchange for sin's captives (like me) and Jesus' resurrection was the ultimate victory over Satan. Satan gets paid and played all on the same weekend!

Inherent in this model of atonement is the serious consideration of evil. Evil is seen as a force in the world that must be dealt with and conquered. It shouldn't surprise us that this view of atonement tends to be dominant during eras of church history when a world power — a dominant nation or group — threatens the principles of Christian faith. This view was widely embraced during the persecutions of the Roman Empire, the period of Protestant Reformation (preached by the Protestants), and during the dark days of Hitler's regime. The ransom theory provided and provides a means of conquering visible evil.

The strength of this ideology, however, is also its greatest weakness. Again, if God is God, why does God have to pay a ransom to Satan? Why does God adhere to a system that gives evil an ounce of credibility when God can create any system God chooses? Why does God not simply abolish evil? In both the ransom theory and the substitutionary theory, God's love and God's power seem to fall short of what I consider God's capacity for both to be. I understand each theory. I just don't understand why God would participate in such systems.

The only explanation that makes sense to me is that Jesus is God's best expression of love toward us. The cross is not an appeasement of God's wrath, but a demonstration of God's love. The cross is humankind at its worst being loved by God at God's best. God, knowing that we carry inordinate amounts of guilt and shame, knowing that we question our worthiness to be called God's children, knowing that we assume God's love to be conditional and God's patience to be short…God, knowing all these things, allowed us to 'do our worst' at Calvary so that we might be assured God will always do God's best. As I said of my children earlier, there is nothing that we — as children of God — can do that will cause God to disown us. If at the cross, we reject and crucify God's greatest expression of love and God *still* loves us, then we can be assured this love has no conditions.

As the Apostle Paul wrote in Romans 5:8, "God proves his love for us in that while we still were sinners Christ died for us." Jesus was God's best expression of love. And in the process of loving us, we learned a lot about God and God learned a lot about us.

Holy Spirit

The Delta Echoes were a southern gospel quartet that appeared at Northside Baptist Church once a year. They always had a limited number of albums available for purchase in the Fellowship Hall after each performance. When that limited number was sold, there was another limited number in the trunk of their car. I looked forward to their annual appearance at our church. I loved the pace of their fastest songs and the familiar blend of their four part harmonies. I loved the predictable final note of every song — a bass note that slid to the lowest tonic while a tenor slid simultaneously up to the same note octaves away. They knew how to stir up the spirit.

My first experience with the Delta Echoes was at our church 'Sing.' These events were held on the fifth Sundays of the months. Sometimes an 'ing' would be added — a 'Singing,' but most times it was just called a 'Sing.' Today it might be called a Christian Karaoke Night. Locals with limited talent would come and croon their favorite gospel tunes. The finale was always a traveling gospel group. Professionals. Sort of. The Delta Echoes were the finale at one of our 'Sings.' The evening was delightful.

My second experience with the Delta Echoes was at a Pentecostal Holiness Church on the outskirts (an understatement) of our little town. This church was way out of town! Out in the woods out of town. It was a fifth Sunday night and their church had scheduled a 'Sing.' Our church canceled services in order to support their 'Sing.' (It was on this evening that I concluded pastors scheduled 'Sings' and canceled services for other church's 'Sings' in order to get an evening off from preaching duties every once in a while. It was good for the preacher and good for the church.) My family traveled to the remote rural gathering place, walked in the white clapboard building, found an empty pew near the middle right, and sat down.

Within moments, the little church filled to capacity. The pew, once comfortably claimed by my kin alone, was now home to another family. The dad, mom, and two children had squeezed into the final square inches of available bench and I was wedged between two moms — mine and theirs. My mom was normal enough. The other mom, however, lost it...or found it...or got it...or something...during the Delta Echoes' portion of the service. The tempo had increased along with the decibel level of the drums. We were all standing and clapping in time with the music. She began to shake. No, tremble. And the tremble progressed into a shake. She shook so hard her reading glasses fell off her nose, landed and danced on her flowery-cotton-dress-covered bouncing bosom, while tethered to her neck by a jewel-bedecked glasses chain. Later I learned she was filled with the Spirit. I told my mom I was filled with fear! I've been a little leery of the Holy Spirit since then.

The Holy Spirit has often been treated like the stepchild of the Holy Trinity. We invest a lot of time in public worship and private piety addressing God the Father and Jesus, His only begotten Son. In most religious traditions, however, the Holy Spirit garners a little less of our energy and verbiage. Maybe it's because we have few visual images to serve as a frame of reference. For God the Father and God the Son there are a multitude of human portrayals in print and stone and other forms of art. God the Spirit is most often symbolized as a dove. It's a little harder to relate to.

The limited visual images are overwhelmed, however, by the plethora of visual expressions. The Spirit gets blamed for a lot of human behavior. The shaking mom of fifth Sunday 'Sing' fame was one of many spiritual expressions I have witnessed in my lifetime. Some of my high school friends enjoyed the gift of tongues during their venture into the charismatic movement. They insisted it was necessary for me to receive and express this gift for my salvation to be secure. They laid hands on me and prayed — in and out of tongues — for almost an hour. They even started suggesting I just "try to make some kind of noise." I argued, "If it's a gift, I'm assuming God will give it and I will know it." I never got it. And I'm not sure they believed I loved Jesus as much as they did from that night forward.

I've seen residents of eastern Kentucky slain in the spirit — flat on their backs, trembling on the sanctuary floor. I've watched worshipers in Tennessee hold rattlers and copperheads as they boldly bore proof of the filling of the Spirit. In calmer cathedrals, I've watched the welling of tears, heard the quiet chanting of prayers, and observed the hopeful reception of healing oils and penitent ashes. Some of these expressions are more comfortable than others.

(I've cried tears, chanted prayers, received oil and ashes. I've always passed on the rattlers and copperheads.) Those expressions comfortable to me may not be comfortable to you. The Spirit blows where it wills, and it seems to be just a little more mysterious than its Trinitarian companions.

This mystery need not completely confound us, however. And this facet of the image of God need not be avoided. Setting human claims and particular expressions aside, we can affirm some wonderful attributes of God's oft-neglected spiritual self.

The Spirit of God is always present.

It was suggested to me long ago, by a volunteer youth minister, that the Trinity has an historical expression — different parts of the Trinity are primarily active in different eras of faith history. Put simply, God the Father is active in the Old Testament era. The Holy Spirit is active following the earthly life of Jesus. And Jesus the Son was active for a little over thirty years during the rule of the Roman Empire. In this system of thought, rather than avoiding the Holy Spirit, we should be deeply involved with the only present expression of the Trinity. In this system of thought, Jesus gets gypped on time. I really don't agree with this system. The youth minister was much beloved, great at planning lock-ins, but should have left Trinitarian theology alone. In all fairness, it appeased the inquisitive mind of this seventh grader (for a while) and allowed us to move on with an invigorating game of capture the flag.

Closer to truth, the Spirit of God is always present and has always been present in the world. In the first verses of Genesis, God's Spirit is moving upon the face of the primordial waters bringing order out of chaos. In the days of the judges and kings, the Spirit of God moved in and out of the lives of Samson, Deborah, Saul, and David. Prophets arose because the Spirit of the Lord was upon them. At Jesus' baptism, the Spirit descended upon him like a dove. Believer after believer, Jew and Gentile, slave and free, male and female were filled with the Spirit of God in the Book of Acts. The last chapter of the biblical story and the last chapter of history were written by John the Apostle while he was "...in the Spirit on the Lord's day...." God is always and has always been present and active in the world.

In Psalm 139, the Psalmist asks, "Where can I go from your Spirit?" This is more than a rhetorical question couched in prayer. It is a literal affirmation of faith. It is an accurate description of the Spirit of God. God's spirit dwells everywhere we are: in the heavens, in the depths of hell, in the mornings, at the farthest reaches of the seas, and even in the midst of the darkest darkness. You and I cannot avoid the Holy Spirit of God. God's spirit is always present with us. In fact...

God's Spirit is active in the most unexpected people and places.

It happens fairly often. Many times I'll be attending a religious conference or browsing the revelations of Facebook or conversing with a friend when I find that an old acquaintance has become a pastor. This person is almost always someone I would have least expected to end up practicing the preaching craft because he or she was typically a little wild, a little cynical or grossly disengaged with spiritual thought. But here they are — ordained and donned with vestments. I imagine it was no different when the Apostle Paul was converted and began his ministry. Folks on both sides of the fence — Pharisees and Christians — scratched their heads and thought, "Really?"

God's Spirit is active in the most unexpected people and places.

It has always been this way. In Genesis 6, the world had gone to pot. God wanted a do-over. God's Spirit inspired a man named Noah to build an ark and provide refuge from a deluge for the seed of a new generation of life. Noah, however, is by no means perfect. If the whole world was bent toward evil, Noah only got a top grade because God was grading on a curve! As soon as the flood ended, Noah planted a vineyard, went in his tent, and got sloshed. Then again, that many months in a boat with a bunch of animals might lead one to drink! My point? This is where the Spirit of God works.

In the minds of some ancient men (and unenlightened modern men, I guess), women carried water and carried children. But the story of deliverance is carried on the shoulders of women in the Book of Exodus. In Exodus 1, it is faithful midwives who refuse to follow Pharaoh's edict and murder Hebrew infants. Reacting to Pharaoh's continued effort to kill Hebrew baby boys, it is a mother — not a father — who hatches a plan to weave reeds together into a small basket and push her child into the Nile among the bulrushes, which gives him a chance at life. It is a daughter who watches over her floating baby brother. It is Pharaoh's daughter (breaking rank with her dictatorial father) who chooses to bathe in the Nile with common folks, finds a Hebrew baby boy, and defiantly decides to adopt and care for the child. We may claim Moses as the hero of the Exodus, but God's Spirit was present and active in the lives of a lot of women that made his career possible.

Ancient Noah and a band of Hebrew women are not hard for the average person of faith to accept. We really don't mind God's Spirit working among 'our own.' The reach of God's spirit is much broader, however. Centuries after the exodus from Egypt, Israel found herself enslaved again. In 587 BCE, Jerusalem was destroyed and the Israelites began a seventy-year exile in the land of Babylon. Their stated and held hope was that a deliverer would arise from among them and bring liberation. This had been God's way in the past. Moses, Samson, David, and others each emerged from the tribes of Israel, were empowered by God, and challenged the chains of Egyptians and Philistines and other enemies. Surely God would deliver again. Surely God had already prepared and prompted the heart of the next hero from Israel. But again, the reach of God's Spirit is much broader.

So the prophet Isaiah startles the hopeful, enslaved Israelites when he identifies the next spirit-filled deliverer.

Here is my servant, whom I uphold, my chosen, in whom my soul delights; I have put my spirit upon him; he will bring forth justice to the nations. (Isaiah 42:1)

Thus says the Lord to his anointed, to Cyrus, whose right hand I have grasped to subdue nations before him and strip kings of their robes to open doors before him — and the gates shall not be closed: "I will go before you and level the mountains, I will break in pieces the doors of bronze and cut through the bars of iron, I will give you the treasures of darkness and riches hidden in secret places, so that you may know that it is I, the Lord, the God of Israel, who call you by your name. For the sake of my servant Jacob, and Israel my chosen, I call you by your name, I surname you, though you do not know me." (Isaiah 45:1-4)

Woe to you who strive with your Maker,
earthen vessels with the potter! Does the
clay say to the one who fashions it, "What
are you making?" or "Your work has no
handles?" Woe to anyone who says to a
father, "What are you begetting?" or to a
woman, "With what are you in labour?"
Thus says the Lord, the Holy One of
Israel, and its Maker: "Will you question me about my children, or command
me concerning the work of my hands? I
made the earth, and created humankind
upon it; it was my hands that stretched
out the heavens, and I commanded all
their host. I have aroused Cyrus in righ-
teousness, and I will make all his paths
straight, he shall build my city and set my
exiles free..." (Isaiah 45:9-13a)

Cyrus would be the next deliverer of Israel. Cyrus
of Persia. Cyrus, the Persian foreigner. God's Spirit
was working in people and places that the Israelites
never expected. And God seems to make it clear in
the later verses that Israel — God's clay-fashioned

children — has no business questioning God concerning other children that have been chosen, called, and named.

Isaiah was not the only prophet calling Israel to a broader understanding of God's Spirit's work in the world. Amos also addressed the exclusivity that seemed to pervade Israel's self-understanding when he wrote,

> Are you not like the Ethiopians to me, O people of Israel? says the Lord. Did I not bring Israel up from the land of Egypt, and the Philistines from Caphtor and the Arameans from Kir? (Amos 9:7)

We read past this prophet and this prophetic line with ease. But to an Israelite, what a radical concept this must have been! Comparing Israel to Ethiopia or the Arameans...or God forbid, the Philistines. But the biblical text makes it clear. God's spirit was active in people and places where Israel least expected.

This freedom of God's Spirit doesn't slow down in the New Testament either. The Book of Acts is a succession of broadening stories. In Acts 1, Jesus tells (maybe warns?) his disciples that the coming

Spirit would empower them to bear witness of him in Jerusalem, Judea (both of which make sense), but also in Samaria and the uttermost parts of the earth! In Acts 2, the day of Pentecost finds hundreds gathered representing many different languages and cultures. All, however, were recipients of the descending Spirit's message. Moving forward through the Book of Acts, we encounter a Philippian jailor, an Ethiopian eunuch, a Roman military official, and various other gentiles who encounter and respond to the free-flowing Spirit of God. The early Christian leaders often struggled to accept and adjust to the ever-widening boundaries of faith family.

This is an attribute of God's Spirit hard for many modern Christians to embrace. We would like to think that God's work is somehow confined to, completed in, and exclusively for those who specifically and intentionally unite their lives with the story of Jesus Christ. Some will quickly quote John's recollection of Jesus' words, "I am the way, the truth and the life. No one comes to Father but by me." These words are certainly a part of our Christian canon — our sacred literature. Read the sacred literature of Israel, however, and they are identified as God's chosen people. Read the sacred texts of Islam and you'll find that no particular race or ethnicity is considered 'chosen.' God's favor rests on those who are righteous. And of course, we are made righteous by believing and following the instruction of the Qu'ran. I am well aware of what our sacred texts say regarding the acceptance of Jesus. But every sacred text of every faithful people group makes the same claim. Once we have experienced the grace of God — entered into relationship with God — we feel a sense of chosen-ness. We love and value the path that brought us to God. Making that the only path, however, runs the danger of restricting the freedom that the Spirit of God demands. We should and must be witnesses to our faith and faith path. But it is a bit arrogant to believe we have a monopoly on God.

People have been sensing and responding to the Spirit of God for centuries — millennia! A temple has been unearthed in Southeastern Turkey — Gobekli Tepe — that dates c. 9000 BCE! Stonehenge was erected nearly seven thousand years later in 2400 BCE. Solomon's temple was built in Jerusalem around 800 BCE. The Bai Ma Se Buddhist temple was carved into the side of a cliff in 500 BCE. The Subrahmanya Hindu temple in Tamil Nadu, India was constructed around 400 BCE. All of these places of worship where people felt the tug of God and longed for the presence of God existed hundreds and thousands of years before Jesus walked the earth. As Paul wrote in his letter to the Romans, "...since the creation of the world God's invisible qualities — his eternal power and divine nature — have been clearly seen...." We may choose to believe differently, but God's Spirit has been and continues to be active in the most unexpected people and places.

I'm often asked my opinion concerning God's presence in the life and faith of non-Christian religious folk who practice other faiths in this expansive and wonderful world. Our us/them mentality tugs hard at our need to know if others are in or out. If others are saved or damned. If others are drawn by the same Spirit. And if we can credibly claim exclusivity with regard to the spirit and truth of God. My typical answer is, "God hasn't asked me to manage God's covenants." I'm truly not interested in trying to separate wheat from weeds in the world. I've already been told (by another member of the trinity) that I don't have the wisdom or the commission to engage that task.

And when I'm tempted to get too pompous or proud in my assumed Christian exclusivity, I again recall the thought of the Apostle Paul in the eleventh chapter of his epistle to the Romans. Paul defends God's continued love and care of the Jewish people — those included in God's covenant with Abraham. Paul was responding to those who had decided the covenant of God in Christ had somehow nullified these earlier promises made to the Israelite peoples. Paul wrote....

> I ask then, has God rejected his people? By no means! (Romans 11:1a)

> God has not rejected his people whom he foreknew. (Romans 11:2a)

> But through their stumbling salvation has come to the Gentiles, so as to make Israel jealous. Now if their stumbling means riches for the world, and if their defeat means riches for Gentiles, how much more will their full inclusion mean! (Romans 11:11b-12)

But if some of the branches were broken
off, and you, a wild olive shoot, were
grafted in their place to share the rich
root of the olive tree, do not boast over
the branches. If you do boast, remember
that it is not you that support the root,
but the root that supports you. You will
say, "Branches were broken off so that I
might be grafted in." That is true. They
were broken off because of their unbe-
lief, but you stand only through faith.
So do not become proud, but stand in
awe. For if God did not spare the natural
branches, perhaps he will not spare you.
Note then the kindness and the severity of God: severity toward those who
have fallen, but God's kindness toward
you, provided you continue in his kindness; otherwise you also will be cut off.
(Romans 11:17-22)

I want you to understand this mystery: a
hardening has come upon part of Israel,
until the full number of the Gentiles has

come in. And so all Israel will be saved; (Romans 11:25b-26a)

"And this is my covenant with them, when I take away their sins." As regards the gospel they are enemies of God for your sake; but as regards election they are beloved, for the sake of their ancestors; for the gifts and the calling of God are irrevocable. (Romans 11:27-29)

O the depth of the riches and wisdom and knowledge of God! How unsearchable are his judgments and how inscrutable his ways! For who has known the mind of the Lord? (Romans 11:33-34a)

Again, God has not asked me to manage God's covenants in the world. I truly do not know what covenants God has made on other continents and in other hearts. I can share my story through the power of the Holy Spirit, listen to the faith stories of others, and trust that God is working in people and places I least expect.

We do not always sense the presence of God's Spirit.

Ironically, while God's Spirit is present in all places — even places we least expect to find the Spirit — there are still times when the Spirit of God seems absent from our lives. These dark and oft desperate times are not uncommon to people of faith. The Psalmist of the Hebrew Scriptures, on more than one occasion, struggles with the hiddenness of God (Psalms 55 & 89). The prophet Isaiah — one of Israel's greatest spokesmen — acknowledges the perceived absence of God in his life (Isaiah 45). Almost every saint has confessed a sense of God's absence. Every Christian I know who's been a part of the faith for any length of time has admitted the same. God's Spirit is everywhere, but sometimes it is painfully imperceptible.

This perceived absence has often been attributed to disobedience or sin in the life of the Christian. Absence as punishment is often our first stop on the road to explaining the Spirit's distance. Nothing, however, could be further from the theological truth. As people of faith, our sins were forgiven through the grace of God in Jesus Christ. We became children of

God in Christ and God has no interest in abandoning his children each and every time we veer from a legal standard of perfection. In fact, when our own children breach the boundaries of acceptable behavior, our natural practice is to engage the child in directive conversation, not abandon our child and leave him or her languishing in loneliness and questions. My disobedience has most often led to extended conversations with God's Spirit. The absence of God's spirit has more often been related to something other than my behavior.

God's perceived absence is directly related to God's mystery. It keeps God mysterious. A present God — particularly a God present in my obedience and absent in my disobedience — is a controllable and predictable God. A God ever present in every challenge becomes a God who is susceptible to my beck and call. Our God is greater and more mysterious than that. Jesus told Nicodemus, the inquisitive Pharisee in John 3, that the Spirit of God is like the wind. The Spirit blows where it wills. God's Spirit cannot be controlled or directed by human want, whim, or even need. God's Spirit blows where it wills. Absence, then, keeps God mysterious.

This perceived absence also keeps us maturing in our faith. As we mature in our physical lives, our parents are less present in the living of our lives. This does not mean they love us less or that their desire for our wellbeing has diminished in any degree. Rather, as we mature, we are responsible for more and more facets of our daily lives. We handle what we can handle and call on mom and dad when the challenge is too difficult. Even then, parents often limit access so that our growing edges are free to develop and strengthen. When we are infants, our every need is cared for. As we grow older, parental love remains but parental touch is lessened.

Years ago, Elizabeth burst into my study at the church. She was anxious to tell her pastor about God's work in her life. Just months before, she had been through some difficult adolescent challenges. After a series of unhealthy decisions, Elizabeth found her way to my office, then to corporate worship, and finally into the baptismal pool. Her path to faith had been a rough and rocky one and her enthusiasm for the faith was no less dramatic. On this particular day, she plopped into the biggest chair in my office and exclaimed, "God spoke to me today!" I asked her how God had spoken and what God had said.

She continued, in an excited tone, to tell me about a cloud. While driving to school that morning, she had been praying about a particular dilemma in her life. She begged God for an answer; all she needed was a 'yes' or a 'no.' Seated at a stoplight, she glanced into the sky before her. Miraculously, she saw a cloud in the shape of . . . a 'YES.' God had spoken. The answer was given. She rested and reveled in the Holy Spirit's vivid presence in her life. With unfettered excitement in her eyes, she asked me what I thought. I hugged her, told her to be grateful for every hint of grace that comes into her life, and to cherish every answered prayer and every sense of God's presence. Then I told her, "Enjoy the miraculous presence while it lasts." Because sometimes the substantive signs necessarily become less frequent — if not altogether diminished — so that our faith has the space to deepen.

God's perceived absence keeps God mysterious and it keeps me maturing in my faith.

The Holy Spirit provides the gifts necessary for the building of each church.

God's spirit has always empowered God's people to do what is necessary in God's world at the time. In the Apostle Paul's letters to the churches in Rome (Romans 12), Corinth (1 Corinthians 12), and Ephesus (Ephesians 4), he provides what are commonly referred to as 'spiritual gifts.' Some of the gifts are held in common by the three churches and others are unique. It is a regular practice in some religious circles to teach these as *the* gifts of the Spirit — the only gifts needed in the ministry of the church. I'm not certain that was ever Paul's intent. Rather, it's more plausible that these were the gifts provided for that particular church at that particular time in that church's story. There is no need for God's Spirit to be static when the challenges within and without the church are so dynamic.

The gift of tongues and the interpretation of tongues are mentioned in Paul's letter to the Corinthians. Even a casual reading of that letter exposes the need for these gifts in that particular congregation. Some people's prayers and worship languages were not always discernible to other worshippers. For there to be some sense of order and community in the church, these gifts were given and employed. Needs were different in the church at Ephesus. Evangelism is listed near the top of Ephesus' list but appears nowhere in the list of gifts presented to Rome and Corinth. In each of these churches, the Holy Spirit provided the gifts necessary for the building of that church.

The Holy Spirit does the same for us today. It would be too limiting for us to assume that the gifts listed in Paul's letters are the only gifts allowed or needed in local congregations today. The gift of music is mentioned nowhere in Paul's discussion of spiritual gifts. I would miss this gift in the fabric of ministry and worship. My business partner is particularly gifted with technical skills. He easily envisions systems where sound, video, and other forms of media may be used to enhance the life and ministry of the church. Churches heavy in administratively gifted members often need the gift of prayerful discernment to nurture a continued faith in God's Spirit among us. On the other hand, we need the gifts of administration to help us navigate the processes and politics of community.

God's Spirit is everywhere, working in the most unexpected people and places. This presence certainly includes the life of the church where needed gifts are liberally given. The Holy Spirit no longer needs to be the feared and avoided stepchild of the Trinity. It is God's Spirit that works in us and through us as individuals and as a community of faith in our world.

The Church

Today is my second full day in Eudora. The Margaret Tiebel Memorial Library has been an excellent environment for the writing of this manuscript. Ms. Mary Bates, the librarian, has been a gracious host. I, however, am sensing a need to connect. I've moved from being alone to being lonely.

I've often said, "Let me listen to a preacher preach three times and I'll tell you what his or her primary issue or problem happens to be." I'll go ahead and tell you mine; I'll spare you the trouble of listening to three of my sermons. My primary issue — my primary problem — is loneliness. You may have already noted this in the prior chapters of this book. Loneliness drives much of my thought about faith.

I came to Eudora, Arkansas a lonely child. I rode in the backseat of my Aunt and Uncle's (now adoptive Mom and Dad's) blue Buick Skylark. It had two doors, bucket seats and a license plate that read "ANY 959." It's odd the things we remember when we are hurting. My first meal in the Dant home was spaghetti. The forks of a new mom, dad, brother, and sister twirled against their plates as they spun the noodles for safe travel to the mouth and subsequent consumption. I just moved the noodles around on my plate. I was surrounded by people, but felt very alone.

In the weeks and months that followed, I created my own contexts for entertainment. I would sit in my clothes closet and play with toys because it felt safer than the open space available in the bedroom or living room. While riding in the backseat of the Buick Skylark, I would conjure extended narratives in my mind. Whether a short trip to the grocer or a longer trip to a neighboring town, I could imagine myself solving a crime, cleaning up a town in the wild west, rocketing to a distant planet, or accompanying Jacques Cousteau on his next undersea adventure. My stories were elaborately detailed, mentally engaging, and created a host of characters for me to befriend. These mental adventures occupied my lonely mind and rescued me from the emotionally restrictive environment I now called home. When spare time was not spent playing or daydreaming, I would stare out the window of my bedroom...for hours...and just feel lonely. I was lonely for something or someone or some context that I wasn't quite able to name. Loneliness has always been my issue.

I leave the library to go visiting. I have heard that Lodie is the owner of a flower shop on the main highway. Lodie and I were classmates long ago, so I think I'll stop by. The drive is less than ten minutes. (A drive anywhere in Eudora is less than ten minutes... really.) I hop out of the rental car, walk in the flower shop, see a semi-familiar face across the counter and exclaim, "Lodie! It's me — Jimmy Dant — one of your elementary school class mates!"

She looks at me with kind, but suspicious eyes and responds, "It's nice to meet you, but I don't have a clue who you are."

I share my history with Lodie. She listens intently and politely apologizes for not remembering me. It's okay. I don't mind. In the half hour that follows, I learn about her husband who was a year ahead of us in school, a lot wilder than us in actions, but tamed at some point by his own response to God's spirit. He is now a minister in the area. Lodie is struggling with some health issues, but has found healing, comfort and a huge smile as a result of her faith. We talk about a few other people we know in common. A few still live in the area. Then Lodie gives me directions to Johnette Wesley Crockett's home. Johnette was my fifth grade teacher.

The drive to Dermott, Arkansas does not take me long — twenty minutes maybe. Johnette and I sit in her living room to talk. We are playing that familiar game of 'catch up and remember.' We celebrate common memories of my fifth grade year and tell each other about our current endeavors. Her curio cabinet and walls are filled with plaques and awards that are testaments to a job well done. But woven between the stories and symbols of success are the frustrations that accompany age, declining health, and the disintegration of an educational system she loves, but is now outside her control. Our tearful parting stays with me as I travel back to Eudora to find June.

June was one of my best friends in Junior High School. She was one of the first African-American friends I made after integration. We had every class together, sat together at most pep rallies, and most importantly, she taught me how to 'bump.' The 'bump' was a popular dance during the early '70s. We didn't do much dancing on our side of the tracks in Eudora, but June knew all the dances. We bumped together. I've heard June has retired from the military and moved back to Eudora. I'm determined to bump into her while I'm here.

Having no idea where to start looking, I've driven onto the main street of town. The only store that appears open is the pharmacy. I step inside and chat with the lady at the register — Carol. She is a polite lady who remembers my family, is intrigued by my presence, and is intent on mentioning every human being she can remember that I might remember. She has no idea who June is or where she lives.

As I step outside to aimlessly continue my adventure, I notice the tire is low on the rental car. About a hundred yards down the street are a couple of African-American gentlemen sitting outside what looks like a garage. I pull over and show them the tire. It is aired in a moment. I'm just about to hop in and drive away when I ask if they know June. Of course they do! Directions are given and I am on my way.

June lives on a street parallel to Highway 65. I drive by her house, but no automobile is in the driveway. I stop to get gas, drive by again and still no car. I drive down Main Street one more time — just because — and then loop by June's. I feel like a stalker. I loop the block one more time and her car is finally in the driveway. She is standing beside it.

The reunion is a happy one. She knows me right away. We hug and laugh and talk. June is caring for an aging mother. She also has a deep concern for the local economy and education systems. She has moved back to Eudora because she cares for the town and its people. I feel cared for. Tomorrow we plan to drive to Lake Village and eat lunch.

I'm back at Harlow's Casino and Resort in Greenville, Mississippi. It's a thirty-minute drive from Eudora, but certainly the nicest accommodations in the area. There's no poker tournament tonight, so I'll be spending the evening in the room. I call my best friend. Every morning and every evening — alone in a hotel room across the river — I call my best friend. In the mornings I share my agenda and know that someone is walking alongside me during the day. In the evenings, I call to give a report and know that I am known. There is a witness to what the day has held.

I'm an introvert that still needs to be connected. I need to know that I am known. Don't get me wrong; I like being alone. I do not enjoy being lonely. It's my issue.

Heavenly Loneliness is healed in the church.

We are lonely for heaven. I'm not referring to a city in the sky where angels flit from cloud to cloud and pluck eternal melodies on golden harps. I'm dreaming with the prophets of a new heaven and new earth. It is a place where God dwells with God's people in undimmed, perfect light. It's a place where all that divides us is reconciled; the lion lies down with the lamb, the child sits near the viper, and Hitler sits at the heavenly feast with the Jews, weeping and welcomed. In fact, it's a place where all tears will finally cease because our conflicts and our pains will have been reconciled. The work we could have done on earth — should have done on earth — will be honestly engaged and completed. It's a place where we no longer see through a glass darkly. We know others and we are known — really known. Finally, we understand.

Heaven is God with us. For many, this one fact is probably enough to describe and define heaven — being in the presence of God. We get a taste of God's presence in the church. Jesus promised us that where two or three are gathered, he would be there. On the night of his betrayal, Jesus lifted bread and wine and claimed they were his body and his blood. When we gather to share the meal, he is there. Jesus taught us that when we love and minister to and among the least of these, we are loving and ministering to him; he is there. As the church worships, shares communion and embraces the people of God's world, it knows the presence of God. Our heavenly loneliness is being healed.

Even within the church, our senses and experiences of God's presence will differ. It has always been this way and probably always will be. In recent years, local congregations have endured divisive 'worship wars' because competing factions within the church believe God should be experienced in a particular way. On the one extreme, traditional liturgy must be maintained. On the other extreme, contemporary expressions are infused into the holy hour. For some people, God is transcendent and must be revered. For others, God is close and must be held. How do we live with differing experiences of the presence of God?

How quickly we forget there are two creation stories in the book of Genesis. In Genesis 1, a transcendent God simply speaks and worlds are formed. A beautiful litany of seven days births creation and all that is in it. It is a formal, reverent image of God. But in Genesis 2, God comes down to earth, sticks his hand in the dirt, forms the shape of a man, places his mouth on the man's nostrils, and breathes the breath of life into him. In the second story, God is close enough to touch. I used to wonder why the editors of Genesis retained two different stories of creation. One could have easily been eliminated or the two could have easily been merged. Maybe they were held separately in order to remind us that our varying experiences of God are valid. They were both retained to offer an opportunity for us to understand each other and live in reconciled community with one another even if and when we differ. What we hold in common is our loneliness for God — our desire to know and be with God. We are lonely for the presence of God.

This heavenly healing, as impossible as it may seem — occurs in the life of the church. We weekly pray, "...Thy kingdom come, Thy will be done, on earth as it is in heaven..." and then we work at being the kingdom. We gather and trust that God will be present with us, reconciliation will occur and we will know communion with one another — a little taste of heaven on earth, the church.

It's not just our heavenly loneliness that is healed, however. I have to believe that somehow God is graced by our presence. Is God acknowledged as God if there is no one to acknowledge him? God chooses to need us. We hear hints throughout the scriptures...

...the Lord takes delight in his people; (Psalm 149:4)

...all things have been created through him (God) for him. (Colossians 1:16)

In Genesis 8:21 and Philippians 4:18, there is reference to God enjoying the pleasing aroma of the sacrifices we make to him. God inhales our praises and adorations the way I enjoy the compliments and gifts of my children. I've saved cards, notes and pictures they've written and drawn through the years. I cherish past conversations. I revel in the memories of challenges conquered. My children are on their own now. I give them space — free will and freedom — to be who they are. But I do love seeing them and talking to them when the opportunities arise. I miss them. There is a heavenly loneliness on the part of

God that is remedied in the gathered, worshiping church. Why else would God be so gracefully persistent? Surely God's persistence is not for pity. More likely, it's to appease God's own loneliness. It is for love.

Human Loneliness is healed in church.

I need you. There, I said it. I need you.

There are many reasons for our human loneliness — my human loneliness. We truly are the children of God. We honestly have God's holy DNA flowing through our very beings. We are good. But, children get hurt. Children hold divergent opinions that lead to arguments. Children bump against the hard edges of maturing. Children make faulty decisions. These hurts, arguments, growing edges, and mistakes can lead us to loneliness. They have the capacity to naturally separate us from each other or they may serve as our excuse for intentionally isolating our selves from each other. Either way, we end up lonely.

Are these things really the cause of my loneliness? Other people suffer the same human condition — the same maladies — and seem healthy and happy. I'm not sure it's my pain, arguments, growing edges, or decisions that in and of itself makes me lonely. In all honesty, it's my desire to take care of these things on my own. It's my independent streak that assumes I can carry these things for a lifetime. And if I can't do it alone, I'll depend on Jesus. But I'm not going to allow another human being to hold my raw, vulnerable pains, opinions, growing edges, and decisions. I don't need you. The result? I'm lonely.

I need you. There, I said it. I need you.

Community is an essential part of humanity. Adam was lonely and needed the companionship of Eve. Moses was fearful and needed the collegial support of his brother Aaron. David was befriended in the struggles of his life by Jonathan. Elijah wept that he was the only prophet left until God reminded him of many more who shared his burden and mission. When Mary experienced the miraculous conception of Jesus, she went to the home of Elizabeth — another woman experiencing a miraculous pregnancy; someone with whom she could experience understanding and community. Jesus surrounded himself with twelve close associates and also valued friendship found in the home of Mary, Martha, and Lazarus. The Apostle Paul never journeyed alone, but always had Barnabas, Timothy, Titus, or Silas by his side. I'm not sure who I think I am, trying to forge ahead in life alone. This is not the way of the faithful. Never has been. Never will be. Community is an essential part of humanity.

Almost every Christian I know can quote Philippians 4:13, "I can do all things through Christ who strengthens me." While it overtly expresses a dependence on Christ, it is also rife with independence. I can do…I can…I. Very few Christians have memorized the next verse, Philippians 4:14. Do you know it?

In any case, it was kind of you to share in
my distress. (Philippians 4:14)

The independent tones of what 'I can do' in Christ are tempered by my need for you. This human loneliness is healed in the church.

In baptism, we die to this life and are raised to new life 'in Christ.' We become a part of the Body of Christ. It is obvious that we cannot be the Body of Christ alone. We bring to this body our particular gifts and weaknesses, in the same way that parts of any physical body have particular abilities and limits. We learn to work together. We accomplish tasks together.

141

Some push and some pull. Some work in a moment while others rest in a moment only to exchange roles as circumstance and need dictate. Our baptism reorients our independence to a mutual dependence upon those in the church. It is in this way that we best reflect the image of God.

In prior chapters, I've referred to our reflection of the image of God as an individual feature. Each of us is created in the image of God and resembles God in some way. It is truer to state that we best reflect God's image corporately as a communion of believers. This is because God dwells in communion with God's self. God exists as a Trinity in union with the Son and the Holy Spirit. God is 'one' in communion. As individuals it is impossible for us to accurately reflect the image and nature of God. But when we are 'one' in Christ, in union with one another, we more fully embody the essence of God. We are the Body of Christ. And as a body, we are never alone.

In the life of the church, we heal heavenly loneliness and human loneliness. If this sounds vaguely familiar, it's the fulfillment of God's greatest commands, greatest calls, and greatest invitations in our life. Love the Lord your God with all your heart, soul, mind, and strength — heavenly loneliness healed.

Love your neighbor as yourself — human loneliness healed.

I need God. I need you. I need the church.

The World

I must admit, I've always had a fascination with what the church calls 'the world.' In the religious contexts of my childhood — church and home — 'the world' was something you avoided; it was verbally disdained. The world held immense and magical influences that could push, draw, tempt, and turn one to the dark side. I was taught to avoid the world. I must admit, however, I've always had a fascination with the world.

I visit the Eudora bank today. During my Junior High school years, I held an afternoon job there — dust mopping floors and emptying garbage cans. It afforded me just enough spending money to get in trouble. I slowly walk through the remodeled building. Walls have been moved, teller cages are modernized, and the side door facing Armstrong Street has been filled and made part of the wall. I don't mind most of the changes…but I miss the side door.

As a young teenager, I would stand at the side
door of the bank leaning on the end of my dust mop
and stare at the pool hall across the street — the only
place in town where beer was served, billiards were
racked, and cards were dealt. I watched the men
come and go. Those who entered walked a little more
steadily than those who exited. When the blackened
glass door swung open, I could catch a glimpse of
neon beer signs and the edge of a pool table. I would
stand for moments on end, waiting for the door to
swing open.

I leave the bank and drive north on Main Street.
I slow and look to the left, just at the edge of down-
town, and fix my attention on one of the dilapidated
buildings at the edge of the block. It was the one place
in town my parents had forbid me go. But, I rode
my bicycle to that building on more than one occasion. I always parked my bike in back and slipped
into the front door as quickly as possible. The smell
of burning incense filled the air, black light posters
covered the walls, and albums and 45s were stacked
in bins. I bought my first 45 in that 'worldly' shop
— "Shambala" by Three Dog Night (with money
I earned from the bank…just enough to get me in
trouble). It was the first of many.

I was in seventh grade when I began playing guitar. It was never enough to simply listen to music. I had to make music — the 'bad kind.' My parents were opposed to me owning the voluptuously shaped instrument and I think would have preferred that I learn the heavenly tones of "Amazing Grace" rather than the tunes I was caressing beneath my fingertips. "South City Midnight Lady," "Night Moves" and "Tequila Sunrise" were a part of my early repertoire.

While I immersed myself in a lot of childhood pleasures considered questionable at the time by my religious context, other worldly ventures were postponed until I was free of parental reach. I was a ripe old forty years of age before I drank a beer...forty-five when I began riding motorcycles and forty-seven when I gathered enough guts to buy a convertible. While I did not live with my parents that long, it's amazing how their internal reach continued to taunt me even when there were miles between us. And, it's amazing how docile my 'worldly ventures' were compared to some of my companions! But, I grew up being told these things were 'of the world.' I carried guilt into a lot of good places.

This year, at fifty-one years of age, I began to find my way to tournament poker tables. And who knows what 'worldly' adventure I'll embark upon next year! I've always struggled with the isolationist posture of some people of faith. Their division between the sacred and secular has never made much sense to me. I allowed it to restrict much of the early movement of my life, but I never understood it. Being 'against certain things' in the world seems to be a poor defining element of faith.

Even more uncomfortable for me than being against certain things, is being against certain people. An us/them posture is quite common among many Christians although it does not reflect the way of Jesus. I've never imagined Jesus separated from the world. He always seemed to be right in the middle of it. I'm pretty sure that's where we've been called to be…at least some of us if not all of us. But, our tendency is to gather amongst ourselves.

Of course, not all gathering is detrimental. In the gathered circles of our family, friends and communities, we find and experience encouragement, strength, comfort and solace. But, this good gets skewed when we start to become too exclusive. I think we gather and group-up for two primary reasons: to *integrate* ourselves into a particular community, tribe, or family (call it what you like) that shares our particular values and views and to *isolate* ourselves from those communities, families, or tribes that do not share our particular values and views. The integration is a good thing. But again, the good of gathering gets skewed when we become too exclusive, and when we are riddled with boundaries. This skewed approach to gathering is evident when Christians assemble and isolate themselves from the world. And once isolated from the world, we Christians will often construe more boundaries, elevate more differentiations and begin to posture ourselves against *each other* based upon theology and practice or both.

I do not believe this incessant and exclusive gathering to be God's primary purpose for us. First of all, it does not reflect God's attitude and actions in the world. The most oft memorized Bible verse in children's Sunday School is John 3:16. "For God so loved the world, he gave his only begotten son, that whosoever believeth in him should not perish but have everlasting life." And speaking of God's only begotten son, this son was — in Christian theology — the very incarnation of Holy God. God with us. God present in 'this world with us.' Or as the Apostle Paul explains it in his letter to the Philippian church, this is a God that chose to empty himself of all heavenly stuff and pour himself into the stuff of the world. And when he did, God — in the form of Jesus — spent his time with tax collectors, prostitutes, lepers, and fishermen. God spent God's earthly life immersed in the world.

And secondly, God has more often encouraged us to scatter. Don't get me wrong, where two or three gather, Christ is there. At the end of the age all the nations shall gather at God's symbolic holy mountain to worship and praise God. At the heavenly feast, all of God's creation will gather to party eternity away in heaven. As we've already stated, gathering is good. God is not completely against our gathering. But in the everyday living and conveying of our faith, we were meant to engage, enjoy, and enhance this world...like salt. We were meant to balance our gathering with scattering into the world.

We see the clash between our disposition and God's desire throughout the biblical text. How often have we heard ministers and teachers assure us Adam and Eve's consumption of the forbidden fruit was the 'original sin.' Not so! This was not humanity's first act of disobedience! The first commandment given by God was "...be fruitful and multiply and fill the earth." The very first humans gave away our nature.

Rather than scattering, they just hung out in the garden! One wonders if they would have *ever* scattered had it not been for the forbidden fruit and God pushing them out into the world! And just chapters later — when the primordial biblical community had grown to become a significant population — our ancestors gathered at Babel to build a tower to heaven. Once again, God had to scatter them and push them out into the world. And lest we think this is an exclusively Old Testament phenomenon, Jesus tells his disciples in Acts 1 to be his witnesses in Jerusalem, Judea, Samaria, and the uttermost parts of the earth. Later in the same book — on more than one occasion — word of God's work in the world is delivered to the disciples *who are in Jerusalem!* Many of them never got out of town! They gathered but they never scattered.

Loving the world is difficult to do if you stand apart from it. The challenge for people of faith as they live is to do two things at once — gather *and* scatter. It is the scattering that keeps us connected to God's world in which we live. And once we appropriately choose to be in the world — connected to the world, we must then decide how to relate to the world. This requires us to overcome the temptations to isolate ourselves from those whose values and views differ from ours. In addition to what might be quiet isolation, we often have to battle the desire to *negatively* engage the world.

I've spent most of my life involved in Sunday worship and Sunday school. Beyond the life of the local church, I've spent a decade or more attending multiple seminaries. So, who would have thought my greatest lesson in theological praxis — how I live my faith in the world — would come from a country music songwriter?!?

I was participating in a conference in Nashville, Tennessee a few years ago. A Bluebird Café Night was presented for the conference attendees one evening. Four songwriters from the Nashville area brought their instruments and lyrics to our intimate gathering and shared an evening with us. One of the musicians presenting was Allen Shamblin. Shamblin is probably best known for co-writing Bonnie Raitt's 1991 hit "I Can't Make You Love Me" and Miranda Lambert's Grammy Award winning "The House that Built Me." I know him, however, for a few offhand words he spoke on Bluebird Café Night. In the space between songs where songwriters tell their stories, in a moment of thoughtful frustration, Allen said,

"Why do people always feel they have to condemn what people do or condone what people do? Why can't we just live compassionately with one another?" It was one of those moments when someone voices exactly what you've felt in a way you've never been able to voice it. Those words have become the theological crux of my faith practice.

We have not been called to condemn the world.

I have heard the same sermon numerous times. I've heard it in multiple states and on varying frequencies of the AM and FM radio dial. Rural radio preachers must have a book from which they pull the sermon. It's almost word for word without failure every time and the congregational response is just as similar. The only real difference is the geographic setting and references.

I was driving from Greenville, South Carolina to Macon, Georgia after a Sunday morning speaking engagement. Deciding to engage one of my stranger hobbies, I scanned the lower frequencies of the FM radio dial until I found the loudest, wind-sucking preacher I could find. I settled on a doozy. He was loud and mad! Just seconds into the sermon, I knew this was 'the sermon.' This time, Atlanta, Georgia — that big city just across the state line — was the culprit. Screaming at a congregation I imagined to number less than a hundred, he berated all the adulterers and fornicators that lived in Atlanta. His angry voice crescendo-ed as he screamed about God casting down the fires of heaven on that pagan city, judging all the fornicators and adulterers gathered there and banishing them to burn forever in the fiery flames of the Devil's hell! As his voice hit the last note of the line, his fist slammed onto the pulpit — almost shaking my little Volkswagen Beetle — and his congregation burst into applause.

Now I have a couple of problems with this sermon. First of all, I'm not sure all the adulterers and fornicators in Georgia and South Carolina are congregated in Atlanta! I've lived in Macon, Georgia for sixteen years. I've visited several cities and towns in both states. And while I'm not taking names or keeping a list, I'm pretty sure there are more than a few sinners scattered around the rest of the two states! My second problem with this all too familiar broadcast is that I'm not sure I could ever cheer or applaud over anyone feeling the judgment of God. I can't get happy about the idea of eternal damnation.

While my radio friend takes condemnation to the extreme, this is a primary approach among some Christians when engaging the world. We often condemn the world.

We have not been called to condone the world.

If we stick with the subject of sexuality as our example, it's easy to see that others are often tempted to move in the opposite direction of condemnation and completely condone the culture around us. After all, who are we to judge? Who among us has not sinned? And isn't much of what we call sin actually just social norms that have little if any biblical basis?

While attending Georgia State University in Atlanta, Georgia, I took a course titled — *Sexuality and Human Relationships.* It was an elective in the Psychology Department — my undergraduate major. (Yes, I made an A.) The professor was an agnostic — a cynical Christian at best. During his lecture on 'Faith and Sexuality,' he made it clear that there was no biblical norm for appropriate sexual relationships. For him, when it came to some issues — like family values and sexuality — the Bible was all over the map! Abraham married his half sister, Jacob had children by two wives and two maids, Solomon had 300 wives and 700 concubines and the Apostle Paul broke stride with all these guys and encouraged people to stay single rather than marry. The professor's point was simply this — whatever norms we embrace with regard to marriage and sexuality, they are probably more reflective of our present culture's values than any standard upheld by our biblical forefathers and foremothers. His conclusion was, that if sexual practice is going to be based on biblical precedent, then we might as well condone just about anything.

A host of factors cause many Christians to simply shrug their shoulders and condone whatever happens in the world. These include: a critical view of scripture, the more pronounced and public expressions of sexuality in our culture (current practices have always existed, they're just more visible today), and the economic realities faced by young adults and senior adults (making cohabitation a more viable option).

This condemning and condoning reaches into a multitude of other modern dilemmas. Drug and alcohol use? It's a question of legalization or harsher controls and penalties. Immigration? How loose or how tight will our borders, policies, and punishments be? And the list goes on and on and on...

We condone or we condemn. Neither option has ever felt completely comfortable for me.

So my mind goes back to the country lyricist, sitting on a stage in Nashville, Tennessee, who pondered between songs and asked, "Why do people always feel they have to condemn what people do or condone what people do? Why can't we just live compassionately with one another?" It is a question that has shaped the framework of my personal faith practice in the world. It is a helpful question for the church to ask. It calls us back to what I believe is the essential Christian task in the world.

We have been called to live compassionately in the world.

We have not been called to condemn or condone the world and one another. We have been called to live compassionately. By compassion, I mean to walk with, live with, seek to understand, and truly love our fellow humans on this journey. I mean to come alongside people's lives as a true friend and trust God to do God's work within them. Do I need to write that again? We simply come alongside our fellow human beings and God does God's work inside them.

This was Jesus' way in the world. This is why I believe so many folk gathered around him. He did not condemn or condone those he came alongside. He lived compassionately with them and trusted God's work in their lives. Zacchaeus was a wee little man and a wee little man was he. Jesus called him down from a sycamore tree but did not 'call him down' for his shady financial practices. Jesus just asked if he'd like to eat lunch. And they did. As the story is told, Jesus neither pointed out Zacchaeus' shortcomings and shortchanging of his clients, nor did Jesus help him justify his business-savvy, profitable methods. Jesus just had lunch with him and allowed God to do God's work in his life. An adulterous woman was brought to Jesus. Jesus knew what she had been accused of doing. Jesus knew the law. But Jesus chose compassion rather than condemning or condoning. Another woman of supposed ill-repute washed and kissed Jesus' feet in the home of Simon the Pharisee. Simon thought to himself, "If Jesus knew what kind of woman she is, he wouldn't let her touch him!" Jesus, however, did not condone or condemn the woman. He did not condone or condemn Simon! He was with them both. He knew, understood, and loved them for who they were in that moment.

Jesus had compassion on them. Jesus did not stand and gaze out on the city of Jerusalem and spout curses or fire and brimstone laden sermons toward the people. The scriptures tell us he had compassion on the city. He wept for the city. This was the way of Jesus. This is why multitudes thronged around him.

I was the unofficial chaplain of Hooters restaurant in Macon, Georgia for almost three years. (I know, it's a tough job, but someone has to do it.) It all began at a wedding. One of my parishioners asked one of the Hooters girls to marry him. She said, "yes." They made their way to my office for premarital counseling sessions and eventually made their way to our church's outdoor amphitheater to exchange their vows. It was a unique service. On the groom's side was an army of buddies dressed in lime green and rust colored leisure suits recently purchased from a vintage clothing store. On the bride's side were all her fellow Hooters girls clad in sundresses and covered with henna tattoos. Everyone was barefoot. I was in my clerical vestments...shoed.

Following the service, the manager of Hooters approached me. His eyes were filled with tears. His breath was a tad fermented. He put his hands on my shoulders and passionately exclaimed, "That was the most beautiful wedding I've ever been to in my life!" He continued his complimentary spiel by suggesting I had the ability to relate to the employees of his establishment. He confessed his own inadequacies with regard to listening to, understanding, and dealing with their problems. Like many employees in other establishments — many people in general — his workers struggled with relational issues, substance abuse issues, and other crises of life. He requested a handful of my business cards. In the days that followed, the phone calls commenced. I became accustomed to sitting at a high top table, munching free wings and listening to the struggles of a fellow human being clad in a tight tank top and bright orange shorts. For almost three years — until management and employees all changed — I walked with the employees of that restaurant. I never condoned. I never condemned. I listened, understood, offered friendship, and allowed God to do God's work in their lives.

I've often been accused of being 'soft on sin' and not 'taking a stand' against anything. Well, I prefer to think I'm compassionate. After all, if everyone has sinned and fallen short of the glory of God, I assume that includes me. And if you and I are both sinners, then I can't stand against you — we'd be fighting. I can't stand over you — I'm not your judge. I won't stand below you and be humiliated. I only feel comfortable — Christ-like — standing beside you, walking with you, struggling with you, and gratefully allowing you to do the same for me. Practicing compassion. Trusting God to do what only God can do. When the church begins to live this way, multitudes will come to Christ again. That's what drew them the first time. Not condemnation or condoning. Compassion.

Postlude

Tonight is my last night in the delta. It's Wednesday night. I've been asked to speak at the midweek prayer service at Northside Baptist Church. It will be my first time addressing this congregation in more than thirty years. There seems to be a bit of curiosity concerning where I've been, what I'm presently doing in Eudora, and what this book contains.

Before I speak, a season of prayer is observed. Names of the sick and afflicted are shared. Updates on illnesses are given. Our servicemen and women are remembered. And an informal tally of the number of persons receiving pacemakers in the last month is referenced. I'm taking notes on a notepad from my hotel. I've been staying across the river in Greenville, Mississippi at Harlow's — a casino and resort hotel! Yep, I'm still wondering how much to share with my extended family about the extent of my life.

After almost three wonderful decades in local church ministry, I followed what I perceived to be the nudging of God's spirit and became an evangelist

— at least that's what the folk sitting around me would call me. I travel from town to town, church to church, conference to conference, and speak. On the days in between, I write or nap or listen to music or run or read or…play poker.

When I ended my last pastoral role on a Sunday in February, I wasn't sure what a 'former pastor' was supposed to do on his first Sunday after his last Sunday. What does a Baptist preacher do on any Sunday when he's not preaching? Particularly his first Sunday clear of clerical responsibilities? I decided to go to Las Vegas.

On the first Sunday following my last Sunday as a pastor, I walked into the Poker Room of the Monte Carlo Hotel and Casino and signed up for the casino's No Limit Texas Hold'em Poker Tournament. An hour later, I was seated at the table and the first cards were dealt.

For the next three hours, I fulfilled one of the dreams on my bucket list. I held 'em and folded 'em and lost a few and won a few and won a few more and won a few more. The tournament ended a little after noon. I won! Yep. I didn't place second or third or thirtieth. I won! And just in case you were wondering, I also entered the evening tournament that began at 11:00 pm. (I was interested in determining if my earlier success had been a fluke or a result of beginner's luck.) I placed second in the evening tournament!

Now when I travel to any town I always check to see if there is a casino nearby. I'm not an addict (I know that's the first thing all addicts say), but I do greatly enjoy the game. Harlow's Casino and Resort is just across the Greenville, Mississippi Bridge, less than 30 miles from Eudora. So, as the prayer service proceeds, I'm taking notes on a notepad from the nearby casino.

The time allotted for prayers has finally ended. The pastor has introduced me as Jimmy Dant. His only comment is, "You people know him better than I do, so he needs no introduction." I walk to the wobbly podium, open my mouth, and let the sound of my voice bounce against the cinder block walls of the Fellowship Hall.

In the second chapter of Matthew's gospel, the visit of the magi is recorded. Strange fellows from the east follow a star in hopes of meeting and honoring a newborn king. Making a stop in Jerusalem, they ask directions of King Herod and his advisors. They are directed to Bethlehem. Upon their arrival in Bethlehem, they gift the Christ child with gold, frankincense, and myrrh. Being warned in a dream to avoid another encounter with King Herod, they return home by an alternate route. Herod is vehement! He had hoped to find and finish off the newborn king through the efforts of the magi. In his anger — and in hopes of annihilating any threat to his throne — he orders the slaughter of all male children under the age of two.

While still weeks from Christmas and Epiphany, this is the story I share with those gathered for prayer at Northside Baptist Church. After reading the text, I tell the congregation I found two things dominating this familiar story: 1) life is inevitably filled with wonderful gifts and 2) life inevitably contains profound difficulties and challenges.

Tears well in all our eyes as I recount the gifts I had received in this little church. I tell them they had given me the gift of faith in Jesus through the loving, evangelical voice of Maggie Pearson. I recall for them the ministries of Nina Cheatham and other teachers who had passed on to me a love for biblical literature. I share story after story, memory after memory, of Vacation Bible School, worship services, youth socials, holiday celebrations, and choir rehearsals.

Each of these memories represents the passion for church this congregation handed me years ago. This now tiny band of followers is responsible for my present love of Christ, scripture, and the community of faith. We all cry.

When the tears are nearly dried, I share with them the challenges of my life. I talk about leaving Eudora and Northside Baptist Church after the collapse of my parents' marriage. I walk them through my personal loneliness, the struggles of my children, and the difficulties of congregational ministry. As I conclude my verbal journey, I thank them again for the gifts they gave me. I assure them those gifts were graceful provisions during the course of my life. But, I confess that the Jesus, Bible, and Church I walk with today look much different than the ones they gave me years ago. No one looks surprised, but I'm not sure anyone wants me to explain.

Following my devotional meditation, the congregation asks a series of questions: Where are my siblings? How many children do I have and what do they do? Was I fired from my last church or was it a friendly parting? What other books have I written?

When the questions are exhausted, a benediction is spoken and the hugging ensues. One lady says she wishes I'd stop playing poker. Another says I'm the best preacher she's ever had the privilege of listening to. The mixed messages continue, but a voice has been found and heard.

Discussion Questions

INTRODUCTION

1. What have been your experiences with faith, God, and the church in your life?

2. When you articulate your faith, are there any phrases with which you are most comfortable? Which ones have the most meaning for you?

3. Which, if any phrases have become inadequate in articulating your experience with God? Why?

SCRIPTURE

1. What are some 'conversations' you've had with scripture? What verses have sparked struggle, questions, interest, and/or doubt for you?

2. The author mentions the four 'voices' of scripture — JEPD. With which voice are you most comfortable?

3. What voice is the hardest for you to relate to?

4. Why is it important for us to have all the voices included in scripture, and in our lives?

HUMANITY

1. What does it mean to you to be 'human'?

2. What might be the significance of the idea that God created humans to need each other, in addition to God? Why do you think God would choose to limit God's self in such a way?

3. "Who told you that you were naked? Who told you there is something wrong with the way God created you?" Have you ever felt this way? Is there any aspect about your personality, interests, passions, preferences that other people have made you feel is shameful, inadequate, or wrong in some way? What would change in your mind, heart, and life if you embraced the idea that how you are is created and meant by God to be a good thing?

SALVATION

1. For the author, the Genesis witness that we are created good is the foundation for salvation. The starting point for him is when we remember who and whose we are. Do you agree or disagree with his starting point? Why? What is your starting point?

2. What is your definition of 'sin'?

3. What do you think the author's definition of 'sin' is?

4. Where do you see the concept of 'repentance' in this chapter?

5. Share an experience when a crisis provided an impetus for change in your faith life.

GOD

1. What do you think and how do you feel about the idea that God is mysterious? Gracefully persistent? Not that impressive?

2. Do these attributes make God seem smaller or bigger in your understanding?

JESUS

1. What have you learned about God by looking at Jesus? In what ways has this information
   impacted your life personally?

2. What is most compelling to you about Jesus' life?
   Death? Resurrection?

3. What do you think might be most compelling to
   God about our human experience?

HOLY SPIRIT

1. Share about a time when you recognized or suspected God's Spirit's presence and work in an unexpected person or place.

2. What are some of the reasons you consider when God seems absent from your life?

3. What is the significance of the author's statement that "A present God — particularly a God present in my obedience and absent in my disobedience — is a controllable and predictable God"?

4. In what ways might God's perceived absence be encouraging you to mature in your faith?

THE CHURCH

1. What is the importance of church for you?

2. The author's understanding of church is shaped by his life experiences and issues centered around loneliness. How might your sense of the church's importance or unimportance be connected to your life experiences and issues?

3. The author says "In the life of the church, we heal heavenly loneliness and human loneliness," which intimates a process that people of faith engage together. What difference does it make to consider the church as a community where heavenly loneliness and human loneliness *are healing*?

THE WORLD

How do you hear the author's statement that "We have not been called to condemn the world. We have not been called to condone the world. We have been called to live compassionately in the world."?

Invite Jim

If your church or organization is interested in delving deeper into the ideas contained in *Finding Your Voice: How to Speak Your Heart's True Faith*, schedule a retreat or conference with Jim Dant. Jim leads retreats and conferences directly related to the material in this book, as well as, many other topics.

Other titles available by Jim Dant:

1 & 2 Samuel: Surviving the Tensions of Life

The Truth Is Sensational Enough

Pray the Trail: A Contemplative Walk on the Ocmulgee Heritage Trail

How Does the Church Decide?

One Pastor, Twelve Steps: My Journey through the Valley of the Shadow of Addiciton

For booking information or to purchase other titles, visit www.jimdant.com, www.faithlab.com or contact Jim directly at jim@faithlab.com.

CPSIA information can be obtained at www.ICGtesting.com
Printed in the USA
LVOW13s2235100214

373170LV00015B/510/P